GREAT GHOSTS OF THE WORLD

Also available in Piccolo True Adventure

Aidan Chambers

HAUNTED HOUSES

MORE HAUNTED HOUSES

Richard Garrett

HOAXES AND SWINDLES

TRUE TALES OF DETECTION

NARROW SQUEAKS!

GREAT SEA MYSTERIES

PICCOLO BOOK OF HEROINES

Frank Hatherley

BUSHRANGERS BOLD!

Carey Miller

SUBMARINES!

Piccolo True Adventures

GREAT GHOSTS OF THE WORLD

AIDAN CHAMBERS

Cover illustration by David Roe
Text illustrations by Peter Edwards

A Piccolo Original

PAN BOOKS LTD

LONDON AND SYDNEY

First published 1974 by Pan Books Ltd,
Cavaye Place, London SW 10 9PG

ISBN 0 330 24058 7

2nd Printing 1974

© Aidan Chambers 1974

*Printed and bound in England by
Hazell Watson & Viney Ltd,
Aylesbury, Bucks*

CONTENTS

From the Author

The world teems with ghosts. There's not a country, not a race of people anywhere, that lacks its own often unique collection of spooks and spectres. Having written three books in this series about British ghosts – *Haunted Houses, More Haunted Houses* (both available in Piccolo) and *Great British Ghosts* (shortly to be published in Piccolo) – I thought it was time to look at other places and to gather together some of the fascinating and often chilling accounts to be found around the world.

The hauntings I've selected to pack into these pages are but a few of the hundreds I'd like to have included had I had the space. And I chose these because they are especially interesting in one feature or another. 'The Ghost in Jail', for instance, is quite the most vividly recorded of any haunting of its kind that I've come across, and still puzzles the experts. 'The Bottle-Breaking Ghost of Turin' is a fine example of a poltergeist – one of those invisible ghosts that throw things about and are somehow comic when they're in action, as well as frightening. 'The Mystery Ghost of Amherst, Nova Scotia' is also a poltergeist, possibly the most famous of them all, and certainly one recorded in the minutest detail by Walter Hubbell, from whose account I quote.

But the most terrifying spectres of all in this book

are the vampires. Those half-ghostly, half-monstrous creatures were most at home in mid-European countries; they were never, I'm glad to say, at all comfortable in Britain. Nowadays they seem to be confined to horror films and such-like fictions. Nevertheless, these grisly beings from the shadow-land between life and death occupy such an important and notable place in ghost-lore that, even though many readers will find them too ugly to stomach, I felt I must include some reports about them. So a warning appears at the head of the chapter in which vampires appear: Not for the squeamish. If raw blood and corpses rising from their graves give you nightmares then it would be best to skip Chapter Three entirely!

A pleasanter topic to finish on. I must thank again the very many readers of my other ghost books who have written to me, telling of their own ghostly experiences and of the spectres that legend claims haunt the areas where they live. Many have also been interested enough to let me know their opinions of the stories I've written for their entertainment as well as for their interest. I'm always glad to hear from such kindly correspondents, and should any readers of this book want to send their comments or stories they should address their letters to Aidan Chambers, c/o Pan Books Ltd, Cavaye Place, London SW10 9PG.

A. C.

CHAPTER ONE

The Ghost in Jail: A German Haunting

One windy September night, Dr Henry Kerner, medical officer of Weinsberg jail, Germany, sat in a locked cell with a 38-year-old prisoner, Mrs Elizabeth Eslinger. At 11.30 PM the doctor heard a noise 'as of some hard body being thrown down on the side of the cell where the woman sat; she immediately began to breathe more rapidly . . .' At that moment Mrs Eslinger broke the silence which had lasted for almost two hours. The ghost, she told the doctor, was present in the cell.

Dr Kerner placed a hand on the woman's forehead and commanded the evil spirit – for so he believed the ghost must be – to depart. According to his detailed report, the doctor then heard 'a strange rattling, cracking noise all round the walls which finally seemed to go out through the window. The woman said the spectre had departed.'

Mrs Eslinger had been troubled for many nights before this by an apparition which, she claimed, visited her in her cell. Dr Kerner had tried various treatments to cure his patient of what he considered at first to be a delusion, but had been forced against his better judgement to have himself locked in the woman's cell to see for himself what really did go on there. The inexplicable noises were no doubt a surprise to him, and his attempt to exorcize the ghost by commanding it to leave was perhaps the desperate remedy of a frightened man.

If he thought this extreme measure had succeeded where medicine had failed, he was soon proved wrong. To begin with, Dr Kerner had been sceptical. His experience in the cell undermined his easy disbelief. Something strange was certainly afoot; he was curious to know more, and he began investigating in earnest.

Ghosts, it turned out, were no strangers to Mrs Eslinger. She was, she said, a 'ghost seer' – someone able to perceive things hidden from most people – though until the appearance of the prison apparition, she had never communicated with a spirit. She had never till then received messages. The Weinsberg ghost, however, was very communicative. It was upset, it said, that Dr Kerner had called it evil; it was nothing of the kind. Rather, it deserved and looked for pity, and requested Mrs Eslinger to pray nightly for its repose. It was, it claimed, the restless spirit of a Roman Catholic priest who had lived in Wimmenthal, Germany, in 1414. During his life the priest had committed a number of crimes, the worst of which was that he and his father had robbed his own brothers. Since his death his spirit had haunted the world, ever in despair, making its presence known to the living by moans and groans and an earthy but unusual smell. To Mrs Eslinger, its form was visible and though she could not actually touch it, she said that when she reached out towards it she could feel its fingers icy in her hand, and that after a while they seemed to grow warmer.

Dr Kerner's first exorcism proved ineffective, and so another sitting was arranged on the night of 18 October. A similar scene took place. This time, however, a third person was present to witness the manifestations: Dr Kerner's wife. Again there was the noise of a heavy body being thrown down at Mrs Eslinger's side; again the doctor – more sympathetic this time – requested the spirit to leave his patient in peace. Again a rattling, cracking noise ran down the cell walls and disappeared, not through the window this time, but down the passage outside the cell.

Was it possible that the doctor was being tricked? Mrs Eslinger had been put into a thickly walled cell block which everyone considered completely secure and well-guarded. During the doctor's investigatory visits, the cell door was locked by the warder and all the other prisoners (many of whom also claimed to have seen the ghost) were carefully secured in their own cells. In such circumstances the authorities considered it extremely unlikely, perhaps even impossible, for anyone to produce night after night the peculiar effects heard and seen in Mrs Eslinger's cell without being caught in the act at some point.

By now, interest in the Weinsberg spectre had spread outside those impregnable prison walls. On 20 October, Justice Heyd accompanied Dr Kerner during yet another all-night vigil. Heyd cannot have been too convinced about the excitements to come (or maybe he had dined and wined too well beforehand) for he kept nodding off to sleep. But the doctor, whose curiosity was intense, stayed wide awake.

The doctor's patience was rewarded. About midnight he witnessed an extraordinary sight. A small, shapeless cloud of yellowish light floated in through the glass of the narrow, barred cell window. It brought with it a cold breeze and a strong, earthy smell.

Justice Heyd jerked out of his doze, shocked by the eerie vision his sleepy eyes beheld. Kerner felt as if ants were running all over his face. Mrs Eslinger flung herself to her knees at her bedside and began praying with passionate fervour.

The two men watched the light as it floated up and down. While they did so, they heard a hollow, unearthly moan echoing round the room.

Two months later, on 9 December, Dr Kerner again saw this ethereal light, which, he said, looked 'like a little animal'. This time he was accompanied by Mrs Mayer, wife of the prison's deputy warden. Both heard a noise at the window so loud that they were sure the

glass would shatter. Mrs Eslinger announced that the ghost had entered the room and was sitting on a stool.

Footsteps were then heard, as if someone was pacing up and down, and the cold breeze was felt again. And this time, both Dr Kerner and Mrs Mayer heard the same hollow, inhuman voice that had previously done no more than moan, uttering the words, 'In the name of Jesus, look on me!' At that moment the yellow light seemed to settle round them like a cloud, the footsteps sounded once more, and the voice said, 'Do you see me now?' And at last Dr Kerner did. The apparition stood in front of the window, a ghostly figure dressed in the clothes of a medieval priest.

Several times more during that eventful night the doctor saw the spectre, usually at Mrs Eslinger's side as she prayed. Finally, it came towards Mrs Mayer. She must have been a strong-minded woman for she confronted the approaching figure without flinching and in a clear voice ordered, 'Go to my husband in his room and leave a sign that you have done so.'

'I will,' replied the unearthly voice.

The cell door was firmly locked, as always, but now it swung open, the apparition floated into the passage outside, and the heavy door closed again. Footsteps echoed through the cell block in the silence of the night.

A few moments later the ghost materialized again, standing by Mrs Eslinger's window. Had it done as it had been bidden? The curious investigators wanted to know. For answer, a hollow laugh filled the room.

Next morning, before his wife or Dr Kerner had mentioned anything about their adventures of the night before, Mr Mayer complained that his room door had been standing wide open when he woke, and that he was certain he had locked and bolted it when he went to bed.

Dr Kerner felt he now had enough evidence and supporting witnesses to write a report. He described in it, as straightforwardly as he could, the facts as he had observed them, concluding with commendable restraint and scientific objectivity that whatever had been going on in Mrs Eslinger's cell it was certainly unusual and, to the best of his knowledge, could not be explained by the accepted laws of nature.

The published report excited wide-spread interest among scientists as well as the ordinary public. A stream of expert investigators visited Weinsberg. Well over fifty interviewed Mrs Eslinger and many of them were treated by the ghost to at least one of its party pieces: the rattling of bars in the window (which later proved to be solidly embedded and quite immovable), the hollow voice, the yellow light. Some of these people attempted to reproduce the effects by trick methods. But try as they might none of them could achieve results that even vaguely resembled the hauntings. Two men heard a noise like gravel falling to the ground as they waited to see Mrs Eslinger. On being admitted to her cell they asked the ghost to repeat the noise, which it did. Two physicists, Dr Fraas and Dr Sicherer, said they saw a dense cloud suspended to one side of Mrs Eslinger's head, and during the night of their visit heard a thudding noise and saw the cell door open and slam shut eight separate times.

The idea that Mrs Eslinger herself might have caused the phenomena must have entered many people's heads, and ought to be considered. One occurrence seems to exonerate her from suspicion. Before she was released, the ghost promised to haunt the cell after she had gone. And it did. Two days after Mrs Eslinger's sentence ended, Mrs Mayer was witness to a number of sounds, none of which had been heard before.

According to Mrs Eslinger, the ghost had frequently pleaded with her to go to Wimmenthal after her release from prison, there to pray for the peace of its soul. This she did, in the presence of many onlookers, who testified that, as she prayed, the figure of a man accompanied by two other smaller apparitions appeared before her. As she finished her prayer, Mrs Eslinger fainted. On reviving, she told how the ghost had asked for her hand. Before holding it out, she had taken care to wrap it in a handkerchief. The ghost touched her hand, and when it did so a flame flashed between them. As proof of this, the strangest event of this unusual haunting, Mrs Eslinger offered the protective handker-chief on which finger marks were clearly scorched.

For over a year between 1835 and 1836 the Weins-berg ghost appeared to the imprisoned Elizabeth Eslinger, but despite Dr Kerner's detailed and honest report, the testimony of scores of other witnesses, and the careful study experts have given the case over the years since it all happened, no one, even now, can say with any certainty just what caused the fascinating phenomena that kept people watching night after night in a cold prison cell. If we are to accept what Mrs Eslinger herself believed, then the ghost was indeed, as it claimed to be, the restless spirit of a sinful priest, a spirit that found at last a sympathetic mortal willing to help it find eternal peace.

CHAPTER TWO

The Bottle-Breaking Ghost of Turin

The annoying thing about ghosts, no matter what kind they are, is that they very often fade away as soon as anyone with expert knowledge appears on the scene. Earnest investigators can sit night after chilly night in a notoriously haunted house and hear or see nothing more spooky than the screech of a preying owl outside the window or the skittering sound of a stray mouse as it scampers across the floor. Send the experts away and back come the ethereal apparitions, the raps and tele-kinetic antics of invisible poltergeists. Once in a while, however, expert and ghost do meet, and the resulting account can be fascinating.

One such famous encounter took place when Professor Cesare Lombroso travelled to Turin to investigate an outbreak of eerie noises. Professor Lombroso was a psychiatrist who specialized in treating criminals. He invented the first 'lie detector' machine. After forty years of scepticism about the existence of ghosts he changed his mind when he met a renowned 'medium', Eusapia Palladino, in 1890. The Professor's experiences with the medium convinced him that

ghosts – psychic phenomena – certainly exist; the prob-
lem is to discover just what the phenomena are and
how they are caused. He spent a good deal of the rest
of his life trying to find the answers – the Turin case is
just one of many he looked into. The following account
of this particular case is taken from his own book, *After
Death – What?*

On the 16th November, in Turin, Via Brava, No. 6,
in a little inn kept by a man named Fumero, there
began to be heard in the day-time, but to a greater
extent at night, a series of strange noises. In seeking
out the cause, it was found that full or empty wine
bottles had been broken in the wine cellar. More frequently they would descend from their places and roll
along the floor, heaping themselves against the closed
door in such a way as to obstruct the entrance when it
was opened. In the sleeping chamber on the upper
floor (which communicated by a staircase with the servants' room near the small public room of the inn),
garments were twisted up, and some of them trans-
ported themselves downstairs into the room beneath.
Two chairs in coming down were broken. Copper utensils which had been hung upon the walls of the servants' dining room fell to the floor and slid over long
reaches of the room, sometimes getting broken. A
spectator put his hat on the bed of the upper chamber;

it disappeared and was later found in the filth-heap of the courtyard below.

Careful examination failed to disclose any normal cause for these performances. No help could be got from either the police or the priest. Nay, when the latter was performing his office, a huge bottle full of wine was broken at his very feet. A vase of flowers that had been brought into the inn descended safely onto a table from the moulding above the door, where it had been placed. Two large bottles were broken in broad daylight. Five or six times, even in the presence of the police, a little staircase ladder, which leaned against the wall at one side of the main room of the inn, was slowly lowered to the floor, yet without hurting any-one. A gun moved across the room and was found on the floor in the opposite corner. Two bottles came down from a high shelf with some force. They were not broken, but they bruised the elbow of a porter.

The people kept crowding in to see, and the police during their investigations gave the Fumero family to understand that they suspected them of simulating, so that the poor creatures decided to suffer the annoyance in silence. They even gave out that it had ceased (after an imaginary visit from me), so as to escape at least the guying, if not the damage. I began attentively to study the case.

I made a minute examination of the premises. The rooms were small. Two of them served the purpose of a wine shop; one was used for a servants' eating room, and was connected by a small stairway with a bed-chamber above. Lastly, there was a deep wine cellar, access to which was obtained by means of a long stair-way and a passageway. The people informed me that they noticed that whenever anyone entered the cellar the bottles began to be broken. I entered at first in the dark, and, sure enough, I heard the breaking of glass and the rolling of bottles under my feet. I thereupon lit up the place. The bottles were massed together upon five shelves, one over the other. In the middle of the room was a rude table. I had six lighted candles placed upon this, on the supposition that the spiritual-istic phenomena would cease in the bright light. On the contrary, I saw three empty bottles, which stood upright on the floor, spin along as if twirled by a finger and break to pieces near the table. To avoid a possible trick I carefully examined (by the light of a large candle) and touched with my hand all the full bottles standing on the shelves and ascertained that there were no wires or strings that might explain the movements. After a few minutes two bottles, then four, and later others on the second and third shelves separated them-selves from the rest and fell to the floor without any violent motion, but rather as if they had been lifted down by someone; six burst upon the wet floor (already drenched with wine) and two remained intact. A quarter of an hour afterwards three others from the last compartment fell and were broken on the floor. Then I turned to leave the cellar. As I was going out, I heard the breaking of another bottle on the floor. When the door was shut, all again became quiet.

I came back on another day. They told me that the same phenomena occurred with increasing frequency, adding that a little brass colour grinder had sprung from one place to another in the servants' room, and, striking against the opposite wall, jammed itself out of shape – as indeed I observed. Two or three chairs had bounced around with such violence that they were broken, without, however, hurting anyone standing by. A table was also broken.

I asked to see and examine all the people of the house. There was a tall waiter lad of thirteen, apparently normal, and the head-waiter, also normal. The master of the house was a brave old soldier who from time to time threatened the spirits with his gun. Judging from his flushed face and forced hilarity, I judged him to be somewhat under the influence of alcohol. The mistress of the inn was a little woman of some fifty years. From infancy up she had been subject to tremors, neuralgia, and nocturnal hallucinations. For all these reasons I counselled the husband to have her leave the premises for three days. She went to Nole, her native town, on the 25th November, and there suffered hallucinations – voices heard at night, movements, persons that no one else saw or heard. But she did not cause any annoying movement of objects. During these days nothing happened at the inn. But as soon as she got back the performances began again, at first furiously, but afterwards more mildly. The occurrences were always the same – utensils, chairs or bottles, broken or displaced. Seeing this, I again counselled that the wife absent herself anew, and she did so on 29th November. On the day the woman left (she was in a state of great excitement and had cursed the alleged spirits), all the dishes and bottles that had been placed on the table were broken and fell on the floor. If the family were going to dine, the table had to be prepared in another place and by another woman, because no dish touched by the mistress remained intact. Hence one naturally suspected that she had mediumistic powers, or would have done so if it had not been that during her absence *the phenomena were repeated in just the same way.* That is to say (to be specific), a pair of shoes of hers that were in the bedchamber, on the dressing-cloth, came downstairs in broad daylight (half-past eight in the morning), traversed the servants' room through the air, passed into the common room of the inn and there fell down at the feet of two customers who were seated at a table. (This was on 27 November.) The shoes were replaced on the dressing-cloth and continually watched, but did not move again until about noon of the next day; and that hour, when all

were at dinner, they disappeared entirely! A week afterwards they were found under the bed of the same chamber.

Another pair of ladies' shoes, placed in the same chamber, on the dressing-cloth, and carefully watched, disappeared and were found only after the lapse of twenty days (folded up as if they were to be packed in a trunk), between the mattresses of a bed in the same chamber that had been turned upside down in vain *two days after the disappearance*.

When it was seen that the phenomena continued just the same, the woman was recalled from Nole, and they were repeated with the same continuity as before. A bottle of effervescent liquor, for example, in full daylight, in the sight of everybody, slowly, as if accompanied by a human hand, passed over a distance of twelve or fifteen feet, as far as the servants' room, the door of which was open, and then fell to the floor and was broken.

After all this it occurred to the host to dismiss the younger of the two waiters. When he left (7 December) all the phenomena ceased. This of course makes one surmise that the motive force emanated from him. Yet he was not an hysteric, and was the cause of no spiritualistic occurrences in his new home.

So it seems that the poltergeist worked in some way through the 13-year-old waiter. Was he really a clever conjurer playing tricks for fun and excitement? Or is there something more to this case than stagecraft? What we do know is that poltergeists very often are associated with young people between the ages of about 10 to about 20. But whether poltergeists are mischievous spirits working through innocent teenagers, or are invisible forces that cause noises and objects to move is something everyone must decide for himself on the basis of the evidence collected from the hundreds of cases recorded down the years.

CHAPTER THREE

Vampires Around the World
(Not to be read by the squeamish)

VAMPIRE, says Webster's *International Dictionary*: 'A blood-sucking ghost or reanimated body of a dead person believed to come from the grave and wander about by night sucking the blood of persons asleep, causing their death'. Belief in vampires, the most ghoulish of all ghosts, is hundreds of years old and can be discovered among people all over the world, though most popularly in Eastern Europe and least often in Britain and North America. Details of the belief vary from place to place but the basic idea is generally the same. Vampires are thought to be the souls of dead witches, or of people who have committed suicide, or of anyone whose corpse was jumped over by an animal (a cat especially) or flown over by a bird. An evil spirit inhabits the dead body, which then rises from its grave and keeps itself 'alive' by feeding on the blood of living people while they lie asleep. Having had their blood sucked by a vampire, these unfortunate victims slowly fall ill, and eventually, after some days or even weeks of decline, they die, becoming vampires in their turn.

So a vampire is a contradiction in terms: a living, dead body.

Catching a vampire and laying it to rest is a gruesome, not to say difficult business. Because you cannot always distinguish an active vampire from an ordinary, harmless, living person, you have to track it back to its grave. There you can easily see it is genuine because the body will look healthy and well-fed when it ought to be decomposed and wasted away. Putting an end to the monster is achieved, generally speaking, by one of two methods. A sharp stake must be driven through the vampire corpse, particularly through the heart, pinning the body to the ground. Or the corpse must be burned until flesh and bone are reduced to ashes.

There are more picturesque methods used in some places, however, such as the one recommended in Bulgaria.

Bulgaria's bottled vampire

Bulgaria, according to legend, abounds with vampires, and an ingenious trap has been devised to waylay them. You bottle them. A sorcerer, or ghost-catcher, arms himself with a holy charm – a picture of a saint, usually – and waits in ambush until the vampire passes by, when the sorcerer chases it, holding the charm in front of him. (Vampires cannot abide holy charms, apparently.) At once the monster will try to escape, seeking refuge from the sacred object. Eventually the ghost-catcher drives it up a tree or onto the roof of a house where beforehand he has left a specially prepared bottle in which is some of the vampire's favourite food – human blood. Seeing the irresistible food in the bottle, and anxious to escape the pursuing sorcerer, the vampire makes itself small by whatever supernatural power vampires and ghosts in general possess, and enters the bottle. The sorcerer has only to push a cork into the bottle for the vampire to be trapped. Bottle and vampire are then thrown into a fire and the vampire is thus destroyed for ever. (Why the vampire does not escape from the trap by putting to work for this purpose the same magic as it used to make itself small enough to get into the bottle has never been satisfactorily explained!)

Rather more seriously, though, we do know as a matter of historical fact that, about 1863, the inhabitants of a small village in Bulgaria were so afraid of what they believed to be an attack upon them by many vampires that they shut themselves up in two or three houses, kept watch all night through, and eventually called in an old woman reputed to be a witch, and asked her to rid them of the evil spirits. She did, but only after a night of horror in which howlings and shriekings and dire curses terrified the villagers. Blood was found next day sprinkled inside and outside the abandoned houses, and furniture had been hurled topsy-turvy in all directions. Whether this was really the work of vampires or was perhaps an extreme case of poltergeist activity, or simply an attack by riotous thieves is now impossible to discover. What the incident shows, however, is that in Bulgaria at this time belief in vampires was so strong that such an event could be seriously blamed on them without anyone suggesting any other likely cause.

China and the head of Liu

Belief in vampires has been as strong in China as in Bulgaria and there yet another means of catching them has been devised. You wait by the coffin until the corpse-spectre has left to go about its grisly business. You then scatter rice and peas and bits of iron round about, completely encircling its resting place. On returning, the vampire will not pass over this barrier of strange charms and you can capture it easily and burn it.

China also offers stories as gory as those to be found anywhere else, stories like the one about a teacher called Liu.

One summer Liu was given a holiday to tend his family graves, an important duty to the ancestor-worshipping Chinese of the times before the recent revolution. His duty done, his holiday over, Liu warned his wife that he must leave home early next day and so she rose at cock-crow and set about preparing her husband's breakfast. When the meal was ready, she went to Liu's room to wake him, but when she drew aside the curtains round his bed she found her husband lying across the bed, headless, and not a drop of blood anywhere. Terror-stricken, the poor woman ran to her neighbours crying for help, and they sent for the local magistrate.

The magistrate could find no culprit, and so, needing to show some results, he arrested Liu's wife. Who else, he argued, could have done it? He had no real evidence to prove his charge, but until he had, he locked the poor woman in jail for safe keeping. And there she languished for many months. She might have remained till death itself released her, had not a neighbour been passing a neglected grave one day and noticed that the tomb had been disturbed and the lid of the coffin was raised a little. His first thought was that thieves had broken in, hoping to rob the body of any jewels or valuables buried with it. So he called some friends and together they looked inside the coffin, intending to check that all was well before securing the tomb.

The sight they uncovered made them gasp. A corpse lay stretched in the coffin, its features as fresh and healthy as a living person's, its body covered with white hair. Between its arms was clutched the head of a man – a man they recognized only too readily: the head was Liu's. Again, the magistrate was brought. He ordered Liu's head be removed from the arms of the vampire's corpse. The men tried to do as they were told, but their combined efforts could not budge it. At last the magistrate ordered that the arms should be cut off so as to release the head from their grasp; and as this was done fresh blood gushed from the wounds. Afterwards, the body was burned, Liu's head decently buried, and his unjustly imprisoned and sorrowing widow set free.

Hungary's vampires galore

As recently as 15 February 1912, the *Daily Telegraph* reported:

> A boy of fourteen died some days ago in a small [Hungarian] village. A farmer, in whose employment the boy had been, thought that the ghost of the latter appeared to him every night. In order to put a stop to these supposed visitations, the farmer, accompanied by some friends, went to the cemetery one night, stuffed three pieces of garlic and three stones in the mouth, and thrust a stake through the corpse, fixing it to the ground. This was to deliver themselves from the evil spirit.

By 1912, though belief in vampires was clearly still strong among ordinary people in Hungary, the authorities were less convinced. The farmer and his friends were arrested for illegally tampering with a grave. In earlier years the farmer's action would have been entirely approved of, even considered courageous, a defence of his community against the scourge of a vampire. In those days the highest people in the land played a part in ridding the country of vampires, as this story from *The Phantom World* by Calmet shows:

A soldier who was billeted at the house of a Haidamaque peasant, on the frontiers of Hungary, as he was one day sitting at table near his host, the master of the house, saw a person he did not know come in and sit down to table with them. The master of the house was strangely frightened at this, as were the rest of the company. The soldier knew not what to think of it, being ignorant of the matter in question. But the master of the house being dead the very next day, the soldier inquired what it meant. They told him it was the body of the father of the host, who had been dead and buried for ten years, who had thus come to sit down next to him, and had announced and caused his death.

The soldier informed the regiment of it, and the regiment gave notice of it to the general officers, who commissioned the Count de Cabreras, Captain of the regiment of Alandetti infantry, to procure information concerning this circumstance. Having gone to the place with some other officers, a surgeon and an auditor, they heard the depositions of all the people belonging to the house, who decided unanimously that the ghost was the father of the master of the house, and that all the soldier had said and reported was the exact truth, which was confirmed by all the inhabitants of the village.

In consequence of this the corpse of the spectre was exhumed and found to be like that of a man who had just expired, and his blood like that of a living man. The Count de Cabreras had the head cut off and caused him to be laid again in the tomb. He also took information concerning other similar ghosts: among others, of a man dead more than thirty years who had come back three times to his house at mealtime. The first time he had sucked the blood from the neck of his own brother, the second time from one of his sons, and the third time from one of the servants of the house; and all three died of it instantly. Upon this deposition the commissary had this man taken out of his grave, and finding that, like the first, his blood was in a fluidic state like that of a living person, he ordered them to run a large nail into his temple and then to lay him again in the grave.

He caused a third to be burned who had been buried more than sixteen years and had sucked the blood and caused the death of two of his sons. The commissary, having made his report to the general officers, was deputed to the Emperor, who commanded that some officers both of war and of justice, some physicians and surgeons and some learned men should be sent to examine the causes of these extraordinary events. The person who related these particulars to us had heard them from the Count de Cabreras at Fribourg in 1730.

*　　　*　　　*

Not to be outdone by counts and soldiers, churchmen took a hand in hunting vampires. At the beginning of the eighteenth century, for example, the Bishop of Olmutz ordered the investigation of several alleged vampire attacks in his diocese. In one of the worst hit villages, Liebava, a brave and certainly crafty inhabitant, stationed himself one night on the top of the local church tower, where he kept watch for the marauding ghoul. Just before midnight he saw the creature rise from its tomb in the churchyard below and make off, leaving behind the shroud which had covered it as it lay in its coffin. Liebava climbed down his ladder, took the shroud and returned to his hiding place. When the vampire returned it flew into a rage when it saw that its shroud had gone. Liebava revealed himself and challenged the monster to climb up and retrieve the shroud. The creature instantly came after him but Liebava knocked it smartly down the ladder as it reached the top of the tower, and it fell heavily to the ground. The jubilant villager scrambled down, cut off the vampire's head with an axe and – so the story goes – nothing more was ever heard of the murderous spectre.

Iraq and the sad tale of Abul and his beautiful bride
An old tale from Arabia as told by Fornari in his *History of Sorcerers*

In the beginning of the fifteenth century there lived at Baghdad an aged merchant who had grown wealthy in his business and who had an only son to whom he was tenderly attached. He resolved to marry him to the daughter of another merchant, a girl of considerable fortune, but without any personal attractions. Abul-Hassain, the merchant's son, on being shown the portrait of the lady, requested his father to delay the marriage till he could reconcile his mind to it. Instead of doing this, however, he fell in love with another girl, the daughter of a sage, and he gave his father no peace till he consented to the marriage. The old man stood out as long as he could, but finding that his son was bent on acquiring the hand of the fair Nadilla, and was equally resolute not to accept the rich and ugly lady, he acquiesced.

The wedding took place with great pomp and ceremony, and a happy honeymoon ensued, which might have been happier but for one little circumstance which led to very serious consequences.

Abul-Hassain noticed that his bride quitted the nuptial couch as soon as she thought her husband was asleep, and did not return to it till an hour before dawn.

One night, filled with curiosity, Hassain, feigning sleep, saw his wife rise and leave the room. He rose, followed cautiously, and saw her enter the cemetery. By the straggling moonbeams he saw her go into a tomb: he stepped in after her.

The scene within was horrible. A party of ghouls

were assembled with the spoils of the graves they had violated and were feasting on the flesh of the long-buried corpses. His own wife, who, by the way, never touched supper at home, played no inconsiderable part in the hideous banquet.

As soon as he could safely escape Abul-Hassain stole back to his bed.

He said nothing to his bride till next evening when supper was laid, and she declined to eat; then he insisted on her partaking, and when she positively refused he exclaimed roughly, 'Oh yes, you keep your appetite for your feasts with the ghouls.' Nadilla was silent; she turned pale and trembled, and without a word sought her bed. At midnight she rose, fell on her husband with her nails and teeth, tore his throat, and, having opened a vein, attempted to suck his blood. He fled from her and on the morrow he opened the tomb, burnt her to ashes and cast the ashes into the Tigris.

The living vampire-man of India

According to traditional beliefs in certain areas, some vampires are not spirits inhabiting dead corpses, but are spirits inhabiting the bodies of living men and women. For most of the time these secret monsters live and work like ordinary folk; then, at night or whenever the fit takes them, they fall under the control of their malicious spirit and prey upon their unsuspecting neighbours.

An account of one such living vampire was reported by Dudley Wright to the *Occult Review* in July 1910. Mr Wright took down this strange tale as it was told him by the doctor involved, who claimed that every detail was true.

Some years ago, a small number of English officials were stationed in a small place in the tropics: their residences were about a quarter of a mile from each other. Suddenly, one of the officials fell ill, but the district medical officer was quite unable to trace the cause of the illness. The official in question made several applications to the Colonial Office for transfer to another station, saying he felt he should die if he remained there. At first the application was refused, but the man got worse and became very depressed. He eventually wrote again, saying that if his application for transfer could not be granted he would be compelled to resign his appointment. The application was then granted; he was transferred, and he recovered his health.

About eighteen months later, another official had a slight attack of fever, from which he fully recovered; but after this attack he began to complain of lassitude which affected him until he went beyond a certain distance from his residence. The moment he returned to within this distance he said he felt as though a wet blanket had been thrown over him, and nothing could rouse him from the depression which seized him. He, too, fell into a low state of health, and on his request was transferred to another station.

Shortly after this transfer the wife of the district medical officer, living within the same area, began to fail in health and became terribly depressed, apparently from no cause whatever. Previously, she had been a cheerful, happy woman, but now she became most depressed and miserable. At last, one night, about 12 o'clock, she woke up shrieking. Her husband rushed into her room, and she said she had woken up with a most awful feeling of depression, and had seen a creature travelling along the cornice of the room. She could only describe it as having a resemblance to something between a gigantic spider and a huge jelly-fish. Her husband ascribed it to a nightmare, but he was disturbed in the same manner on the following night, when his wife said she had been awake for a quarter of an hour, but had not had the strength to call him before. He found her in a state of collapse, pulse exceedingly low, temperature three degrees below normal, pallid, and in a cold sweat. He mixed her a draught which had the effect of sending her to sleep.

In the morning she said she must leave the station and go home, as to stop there would mean her death. Thinking to divert her attention, her husband took her away on a pleasure trip, and he was glad to see that she entirely recovered her former cheerful expression and high spirits. This state of things lasted until, returning home in a rickshaw alongside her husband's, her face changed and she resumed her gloomy countenance.

'There,' she said, 'is it not awful? I have been so well and happy all the week, and now I feel as though a pall has been thrown over me.'

Matters got worse, and she became more depressed than ever, and only a few nights passed before her husband was again called to her bedside about midnight. He found his wife in a state of considerable weakness, although it was not so acute as on the previous occasion. She said to him, 'I want you to examine the back of my neck and shoulders very carefully and see if there is any mark on the skin of any kind whatever.'

Her husband did so, but could not find a mark.

'Get a glass and look again. See if you can find any puncture from a sharp-pointed tooth.'

He made a microscopical examination, but found absolutely nothing.

'Now,' said his wife, 'I can tell you what is the matter. I dreamed that I was in a house where I lived when I was a girl. My little boy called out to me. I ran down to him, but when I reached the bottom of the stairs a tall, black man came towards me. I waved him off, but I could not move to get away from him, though I pushed the boy out of his reach. The man came towards me, seized me in his arms, sat down at the bottom of the stairs, put me on his knee, and proceeded to suck from a point at the upper part of the spine, just below the neck. I felt that he was drawing all the blood and life out of me. Then he threw me from him, and apparently I lost consciousness as he did so. I felt as though I was dying. Then I woke up, and I had been lying here for a quarter of an hour or twenty minutes before I was able to call you.'

'Have you ever experienced anything of this character before?' asked her husband.

'No, I have not; but night after night for many months I have woken up in exactly the same state, and that has been the sole cause of my mental depression. I have not said anything about it because it seemed so foolish, but now I have had this definite dream I cannot hold my tongue any longer.'

She soon passed into a peaceful sleep, and on discussing the matter the following morning with her husband she said, 'I have a feeling somehow that it will not happen again. I feel quite well and strong, and my depression is gone.'

In the afternoon husband and wife were going together to their club, when they met a tall Indian, the owner of a large number of milch cattle, and reputed to be a wealthy man. The surgeon's wife suddenly stopped, turned pale, and said immediately, 'That is the man I saw in my dream.'

The husband went directly up to the man and said to him, 'Look here, I will give you twelve hours to get out of this place. I know everything that happened last night at midnight, and I will kill you like a dog if I find you here in twelve hours' time.'

The Indian disappeared the same night, leaving behind the whole of his property. No news had been heard of him five years afterwards. Since his departure no one in that area has complained of depression and lassitude.

The Coffin Lid from Ralston's *Russian Folk Tales*

A moujik* was driving along one night with a load of pots. His horse grew tired, and all of a sudden it came to a standstill alongside a graveyard. The moujik unharnessed his horse and set it free to graze; meanwhile he laid himself down on one of the graves. But somehow he didn't go to sleep.

He remained there some time. Suddenly the grave began to open beneath him; he felt the movement and sprang to his feet. The grave having opened, out of it came a corpse, wrapped in a white shroud, and holding a coffin lid. He ran to the church, laid the coffin lid at the door, and then set off for the village.

The moujik was a daring fellow. He picked up the coffin lid and remained standing beside his cart, waiting to see what would happen. After a short delay the

* Moujik: the Russian word for 'peasant'.

dead man came back, and was going to snatch up his coffin lid – but it was not to be seen. The corpse began to track it out, traced it to the moujik, and said, 'Give me my lid; if you don't, I'll tear you to bits!'

'And my hatchet – how about that?' answered the moujik. 'Why, it's I who'll be chopping you into small pieces!'

'Do give it back to me, good man!' begged the corpse.

'I'll give it when you tell me where you've been and what you've done.'

'Well, I've been in the village, and there I've killed a couple of youngsters.'

'Well, then, tell me how they can be brought back to life.'

The corpse reluctantly made answer, 'Cut off the left skirt of my shroud. Take it with you, and when you come into the house where the youngsters were killed, pour some live coals into a pot and put the piece of shroud in with them, and then lock the door. The lads will be revived by the smoke immediately.'

The moujik cut off the left skirt of the shroud and gave up the coffin lid. The corpse went to its grave. The grave opened. But just as the dead man was descending into it, all of a sudden the cocks began to crow, and he had not time to get properly covered over. One end of the coffin lid remained standing out of the ground.

The moujik saw all this and made a note of it. The

day began to dawn; he harnessed his horse and drove into the village. In one of the houses he heard cries and wailing. In he went – there lay two dead lads.

'Don't cry,' said he; 'I can bring them to life.'

'Do bring them to life,' said their relatives. 'We'll give you half of all we possess.'

The moujik did everything as the corpse had instructed him, and the lads came back to life. Their relatives were delighted, but they immediately seized the moujik and bound him with cords, saying, 'No, no, trickster! We'll hand you over to the authorities. Since you know how to bring them back to life, maybe it was you who killed them!'

'What are you thinking about, true believers?' cried the moujik.

Then he told them everything that had happened to him during the night. Well, they spread the news through the village, and the whole population assembled and stormed into the graveyard. They found the grave from which the dead man had come out; they tore it open, and they drove an aspen stake right into the heart of the corpse, so that it might no more rise up and slay. But they rewarded the moujik handsomely, and sent him home with great honour.

The moujik's tale could well be nothing but an entertainment without a scrap of truth in it from beginning to end. It shows, however, how much the Russians, like other East European peoples, believed in vampires. When the Russian authorities were convinced that a vampire was abroad, they acted swiftly and thoroughly, as this record dating from 1738 proves:

In the beginning of September there died in the village of Kisilova, three leagues from Graditz, an old man who was sixty-two years of age. Three days after he had been buried, he appeared in the night to his son, and asked him for something to eat; the son having given him something, he ate and disappeared. The next day the son recounted to the neighbours what had happened. That night the father did not appear, but the following night he showed himself and asked for something to eat. They know not whether the son gave him anything or not; but the next day he was found dead in his bed. On the same day, five or six persons felt suddenly ill in the village, and died one after the other in a few days.

The officer or bailiff of the place, when informed of what had happened, sent an account of it to the tribunal of Belgrade, which dispatched to the village two of these officers and an executioner to examine this affair. The imperial officer from whom we have this account repaired thither from Graditz to be a witness of what took place.

They opened the graves of those who had been dead six weeks. When they came to that of the old man, they found him with his eyes open, having a fine colour, with natural respiration, nevertheless motionless as the dead: whence they concluded that he was most undoubtedly a vampire. The executioner drove a stake into his heart; they then raised a pile and reduced the corpse to ashes.

Mr Ray and Mr Rose of the USA

Like Britain, the United States of America has never been much given to vampirism. But it has not escaped entirely. On 8 June 1854, for example, the bodies of two brothers, sons of a Mr Horace Ray, were dug up and burned because local people believed the deceased men were feeding on their living relatives, slowly killing them one after another. In 1875, a Dr Dyer, a physician of Chicago, reported that the body of a woman was taken from its grave and the lungs burned, also because the corpse was supposed to be drawing the life out of surviving members of the family. Only a year before, in 1874, and for the same reason, in the village of Placedale, Rhode Island, Mr William Rose disinterred the corpse of his daughter and, according to the report in the *Providence Journal*, cut out and burned the heart.

Yugoslavia and Arnod's gruesome end

It is appropriate that the last country in this alphabetical trip round the vampire world should bring us back to the area where this kind of ghost has always been most deeply believed in. The story which follows was written at Meduegna near Belgrade, is dated 7 June 1732, and is signed by three army surgeons, a sub-lieutenant, and their superior officer, a lieutenant-colonel. It is, however we look at it, an extraordinary and very sad tale.

In the spring of 1727 there returned from the Levant to the village of Meduegna, one Arnod Paole, who, in a few years' military service and varied adventure, had amassed enough to purchase a cottage and an acre or two of land in his native place, where he gave out that he meant to pass the remainder of his days. Arnod had yet scarcely reached the prime of manhood; and though he must have encountered the rough as well as the smooth of life, and have mingled with many a wild and reckless companion, yet his natural good disposition and honest principles had preserved him un-scathed in the scenes he had passed through. At all events, such were the thoughts expressed by his neigh-bours as they discussed his return and settlement among them. Nor did the frank and open countenance of Arnod, his obliging habits and steady conduct, argue their judgements incorrect. Nevertheless, there was something occasionally noticeable in his ways, a look and tone that betrayed inward disquiet. He would often refuse to join his friends, or on some sudden plea would abruptly quit their society. And he still more unaccountably, and it seemed systematically, avoided meeting his pretty neighbour, Nina, whose father occupied the next farm to his own. At the age of 17, Nina was as charming a picture of youth, cheerfulness, innocence, and confidence as you could have seen in all the world. Why did Arnod shrink from meeting her? He was young; had a little property; had health and industry; and he had told his friends he had formed no ties in other lands. Why then did he avoid the fascination of the pretty Nina? But he did so, yet less and less resolutely, for he felt the charm of her presence. Who could have done otherwise? And how long he resisted the impulse of his fondness for the innocent girl who sought to cheer his fits of depression.

And they were to be united – were betrothed; yet still the anxious gloom would fitfully overcast his countenance, even in the sunshine of those hours.

'What is it, dear Arnod,' asked Nina, 'that makes you sad? It cannot be on my account, I know, for you were sad before you noticed me.'

'Nina,' he answered, 'I have done, I fear, a great wrong in trying to gain your affections. Nina, I have a fixed impression that I shall not live; yet knowing this, I have selfishly made my existence necessary to your happiness.'

'How strangely you talk, dear Arnod! Who in the village is stronger and healthier than you? You feared no danger when you were a soldier. What danger do you fear as a villager of Meduegna?'

'It haunts me, Nina.'

'But, Arnod, you were sad before you thought of me. Did you then fear to die?'

'Oh, Nina, it is something worse than death.'

'Arnod, tell me.'

'It was in Cossova this fate befell me. Here you have hitherto escaped the terrible scourge. But there they die, and the dead visit the living. I experienced the first frightful visitation, and I fled; but not till I had sought his grave and executed the dread expiation from the vampire.'

Nina's blood ran cold. She stood horror-stricken. But her young heart soon mastered her first despair. With a touching voice she spoke, 'Fear not, dear Arnod; fear not now. I will be your shield, or I will die with you.'

And she encircled his neck with her gentle arms. Afterwards they found a reasonable ground for banishing or allaying their apprehension in the lengthy time which had elapsed since Arnod left Cossova, during which no fearful visitant had again approached him; and they fondly protested *that* gave them security.

One day, about a week after this conversation, Arnod missed his footing when on the top of a loaded hay-wagon, and fell from it to the ground. He was picked up insensible, and carried home, where, after lingering a short time, he died. His interment, as usual, followed immediately. But what pencil could paint Nina's grief?

Twenty or thirty days after his decease, several people in the neighbourhood complained that they were haunted by the deceased Arnod; and what was more to the purpose, four of them died. The evil looked at sceptically was bad enough, but aggravated by the suggestions of superstition it spread a panic through the whole district. To allay the popular terror, and, if possible, to get at the root of the evil, a determination was come to publicly to disinter the body of Arnod, with a view to ascertaining whether he really was a vampire, and, in that event, of treating him appropriately. The day fixed for these proceedings was the fortieth after the burial.

It was on a grey morning in early August that the commission visited the cemetery of Meduegna, and moved towards the grave of Arnod Paole. The work of throwing out the earth was begun by the old sexton, who lived in the Leichenhaus beyond the great crucifix. Near the grave stood two military surgeons from Belgrade, and a drummer-boy, who held their case of instruments. The boy looked on with keen interest; and when the coffin was exposed and rather roughly drawn out of the grave, his pale face and bright, intent eye showed how the scene moved him. The sexton lifted the lid of the coffin; the body had become

inclined to one side. Then, turning it straight, he said:
'Ha, ha! What? Your mouth not wiped since last
night's work?'

The spectators shuddered; the drummer-boy sank
forward, fainting, and upset the instrument case, scat-
tering its contents; the senior surgeon, infected with
the horror of the scene, repressed a hasty exclamation.
They threw water on the drummer-boy and he recovered, but would not leave the spot. Then they in-
spected the body of Arnod. It looked as if it had not
been dead a day. After handling it, the scarfskin came
off, but below were new skin and new nails! How
could they have come there but from this foul feeding?
The case was clear enough: there lay before them the
thing they dreaded – the vampire! So, without more
ado, they simply drove a stake through Arnod's chest,
whereupon a quantity of blood gushed forth, and the
corpse uttered a dreadful groan.

'Murder! Murder!' shrieked the drummer-boy, as
he rushed wildly, with convulsed gestures, from the
scene.

Arnod's body was burned, as custom required, and
the ashes returned to his grave. The bodies of the four
victims were also staked to the ground and afterwards
burned to ensure they did not rise again in vampire
form. But this was not the end. Five years later an outbreak of vampirism of such violence troubled the
village that the authorities opened every grave in the

cemetery in a hunt for the offending corpses. According to medical documents, of thirteen bodies exhumed, ten were in vampire condition: perfectly healthy-looking, without any signs of decomposition, although all of them had been buried for at least six weeks.

What are we to make of these unattractive ghosts? Are all these stories and the many hundreds more that can be found in records around the world, nothing but tall tales, fictions invented to frighten and terrify? Surely out of so many there must at least in some be a pinch of truth? But what are the facts about these bloodthirsty supernatural beings? Some people have tried to guess and their answers are sometimes plausible; but no one really knows. All we can say at present is that vampires and the stories about them have fascinated people everywhere for many hundreds of years and remain today full of a gruesome kind of interest. It is comforting, however, to know that it is many years since anyone claimed to have been attacked by a vampire; the nearest any of us get to such monsters these days is in a cinema as we watch the lurid adventures of the greatest fictional vampire of them all, Dracula himself.

CHAPTER FOUR

The Ghost-Horse of South Africa

An Englishman was hunting in the Transvaal not long after the end of the Boer War in 1902, when one evening he met a phantom horse. So strange was his experience that he wrote a letter about it to the journalist, W. T. Stead.

I am not a believer in ghosts, nor ever was; but seeing you wanted a census of them, I can't help giving you a remarkable experience of mine. It was some three summers back, and I was out with a party of Boer hunters. We had crossed from the Northern boundary of the Transvaal, and were camped on the ridges of the Sembombo. I had been out from sunrise, and was returning about dusk with the skin of a fine black ostrich thrown across the saddle in front of me, in the best of spirits at my good luck. Making straight for the camp, I had hardly entered a thick bush when I thought that I heard somebody behind me. Looking behind, I saw a man mounted on a white horse. You can imagine my surprise, for my horse was the only one in camp, and we were the only party in the country.

Without considering, I quickened my pace into a canter, and on doing so my follower appeared to do the same. At this I lost all confidence, and made a run for it, with my follower in hot pursuit, as it appeared to my imagination; and I did race for it (the ostrich skin went flying in about two minutes, and my rifle would have done the same had it not been strapped over my shoulders). This I kept up until I rode into camp right among the pals cooking the evening meal. The Boers about the camp were quick in their inquiries as to my distressed condition, and regaining confidence, I was putting them off as best I could, when the old boss (an old Boer of some 68 or 70 years), looking up from the fire, said:

'The white horse! The Englishman has seen the white horse.'

This I denied but to no purpose. And that night round the camp fire I took the trouble to make inquiries as to the antecedents of the white horse. And the old Boer, after he had commanded silence, began. He said:

'The English are not brave, but foolish. We beat them at Majuba, some twenty-five seasons back. There was an Englishman here like you; he had brought a horse with him, against our advice, to be killed with the fly, the same as yours will be in a day or two. And he, like you, would go where he was told not to go; and one day he went into a bush (that very bush you rode through tonight), and he shot seven elephants, and the next day he went in to fetch the ivory, and about night his horse came into camp riderless, and was dead from the fly before the sun went down. The Englishman is in that bush now; anyway, he never came back. And now anybody who ventures into that bush is chased by the white horse. I wouldn't go into that bush for all the ivory in the land. The English are not brave, but foolish; we beat them at Majuba.'

Here he ran into a torrent of abuse of all Englishmen in general, and in particular. And I took the opportunity of rolling myself up in my blankets for the night, sleeping all the better for my adventure.

I don't believe in ghosts, but I was firmly convinced during that run of mine, and can vouch for the accuracy of it, not having heard a word of the Englishman or his white horse before my headlong return to the camp that night. I shortly hope to be near that bush again, but, like the old Boer, I can say I wouldn't go into that bush again for all the ivory in the land.

CHAPTER FIVE

The Stone-Throwing Ghost of Mauritius

At 7 AM on Monday, 21 September 1937, a stone fell on the roof of a bungalow in the rue Touraine, a street in Port Louis, capital of the crowded little sub-tropical island of Mauritius. The stone bounced off the roof onto the paved courtyard below, frightening an 11-year-old servant girl who fled at once into the house for safety. During the rest of this eventful day another forty or so stones were to rain onto the roof and into the courtyard. More surprising, and certainly more frightening for the occupants, at least that number fell *inside* the house and no one could tell where they came from.

Not unnaturally, the owner of the bungalow, Mr Cappy Ricks, supposed the stones were being thrown by mischievous boys. The police were called in and a sharp look-out was kept all day long, without any success. No one was seen behaving suspiciously. The day's bombardment reached a climax that evening when a stone fell vertically into one of the bedrooms, while outside a shower of missiles poured into the courtyard.

This final assault proved too much for the nerve-wracked servant girl. She rushed, shrieking, indoors and flung herself headlong under the dining-room table from where she was rescued in a state of collapse and sent home.

Next day, just after seven in the morning, the assault began again. This time more stones than ever fell, and mixed in among the stones were other objects, too. One in particular caught Mr Rick's eye. About seven inches long, wedge shaped, with a round hole near its thinner edge, it was to become very familiar before the disturbance ended, appearing here and there all over the house. Another of the projectiles was a large iron shackle minus its holding pin (the kind of tool used to link pieces of chain). It had been lying inoffensively in the courtyard for months, yet now it was flying dangerously about without apparent cause.

Again the police were summoned. At least two stood guard inside the house all day, while outside a third found himself a perch high up in a tree from where he had a bird's eye view of the bungalow, its grounds and the surrounding areas. His watch was fruitless. By the time night came and the barrage ended no one had been apprehended yet scores of stones had fallen, many inside the building even though all doors and windows were firmly closed.

The next day, Wednesday, the activity grew worse. In his own account, first published in *The Forum* of

Johannesburg, Mr Ricks set down the details of this appalling experience:

While the cook was preparing breakfast, a large steel nut, that also had lain in the court during the whole of my tenancy, apparently fell from the low roof of the kitchen (the door and window being closed), and dashed a dish to pieces from her hands.

In an outside bathroom I was struck on the shoulder by a six and a half pound stone that had risen from the ground six feet away and entered the small room by a six-inch space above the door that gave it light. The inspector, who at that moment was leaning against a tree about six feet distant, had seen nothing. Only a thick bath towel saved me from injury.

Of the last four stones that fell this morning, one fell on a thin china plate on the dining table without even cracking it, although it had been observed to fall with something of a crash. Another fell between the necks of three bottles standing together on the sideboard: it looked as if it had been placed there with the greatest care, instead of having come to rest after a flight of at least twenty feet. The third stone fell behind me in a corner of the dining-room, and, as I sprang up and turned round, the fourth one fell on the seat of the stool on which I had been sitting. Door and windows were closed and had been for some time. The room was a small one, and there was no heavy furniture behind which even a child or a monkey could successfully hide.

My wife and baby, with the two servants, went to her mother's house, a quarter of a mile away, and the stones went there too, and began to fall.

A retreat was made to a neighbour's house, but the stones followed again, to smash up pot plants and a table, and make a mess of the veranda generally.

In desperation I collected my small family and took them to a hotel, where only three stones fell from noon onwards.

At midday I returned to the house to find the *nan-eine* [the servant girl] washing baby clothes at the out-door tap. I told her to make a cup of tea, and as she crossed the veranda to enter the house I saw a large stone rise of its own accord from the side of the steps to a height of about five feet and make straight for her. She fled into the street and was with difficulty coaxed back to complete her task.

Later, when she was laying the study table to serve the tea, a stone rose over the veranda rail and flew into the house between the partially open swing doors. It was travelling straight at my stomach, and as I stooped to catch it in its flight, it swerved some forty degrees to the right and fell onto the table, to smash glassware and a milk jug and knock to the floor a full glass jar of jelly.

At this turn in the proceedings I came to a decision

– that the *naneine* must leave us, for it had been forced in my notice that the stones fell only when she was in or around the house. But when I called for her she was not to be found. She was bolting for home.

More than three hundred missiles fell in the house and on the veranda this day, including the one with a hole in it which I had already pitched into the court on two successive days; it had become an old friend!

I spent the night in the house alone, with nothing to disturb my rest, but at the usual time in the morning of the fourth day the missiles came as before, inside the house and on the veranda. Though I did not then know it – doors and windows being closed – the *naneine* was at her usual morning task in the courtyard and had been for some time.

In an hour and a half, with doors and windows still closed, fourteen stones, up to five pounds in weight, an unripe melon, and a quantity of seeds fell in the dining-room and the adjoining bedroom. At 9.30, I gathered these up and placed them on the bed with a note for the detective officer whom I had been told to expect at ten o'clock.

I then left for my office, after thoroughly searching and locking up the house. I had to fight my way out of the outer courtyard door, round which morbidly interested people were tightly packed. The *naneine* was at the tap.

I had not been in the office more than a few minutes

when I was called on the phone. Pandemonium had broken out in the house a few minutes after my departure. The police broke in and found the dining-room a mass of wreckage, caused by the fourteen stones that I had left with the note on the bed.

The communicating door had been closed and locked, but the stones had travelled horizontally from one room to another by way of a deep window recess that was common to both rooms, and in their passage had broken a window pane and a medicine bottle, and had torn down the curtains and scattered from the windowsill magazines and journals, that were now lying strewn around the dining-room floor.

Everything of a breakable nature on the table and sideboard had been smashed; also the hanging lamp and the clock.

In the bedroom the seeds were found to have entirely disappeared, and the wardrobe doors, which were perfectly fitting and had been securely locked, were found to be wide open, though nothing was missing. The green melon reposed alone on the bed.

I returned to the office just in time to receive another phone call, this time from the proprietor of the hotel, who, although I was on the most friendly terms with him, instantly demanded that I removed my family at once. There was nothing to be done but comply with his very reasonable demand, exasperating though it was. So I brought my people back to their home – hoping for the best, while fearing the worst.

A minute after leaving the hotel, and while driving through the city's main thoroughfare, a stone rose in front of the car and entered between the open leaves of the wind-screen. It struck one of the party on the shoulder, without inflicting any injury, however, and came to rest on the rear seat. I picked it up. It had a hole in it, and it should have been lying in my court-yard a mile away, for I had pitched it there only a few hours before.

When we arrived in the rue Touraine, it was to find a thousand or more people filling the house, court and road outside. These were quickly dispersed without ceremony, and with them the *naneine* – and not a stone fell afterwards . . .

The experts agree that what happened in Mauritius was not a fraud, nor was anyone deliberately throwing things about inside and outside Mr Rick's bungalow. The disturbance was the work of a poltergeist, that curious physical phenomenon also at work in the Turin case (see page 18) and the cause of the Amherst, Nova Scotia haunting (see page 111). Such events are fairly common all round the world and all down the ages. In *Haunted Houses** I have described one of the most famous, the haunting of Epworth Parsonage, home of

* Also published in the Piccolo True Adventure series.

John Wesley, founder of Methodism, as well as reporting the damage caused in Sid Mularney's motor cycle workshop at Leighton Buzzard in 1963 and the fearsome attack on Andrew McKie's farm in 1695.

The word 'poltergeist' comes from the German for 'noise ghost' and is used to name any phenomenon that makes furniture and other objects move without apparent contact with ordinary people or machines. Rappings and strange noises are also often heard accompanying poltergeist upsets, and, most terrifying feature of all, sudden outbursts of fire. A great deal more scientific investigation will have to be done if we are ever to understand completely what causes poltergeists. Meanwhile, year after year, new events are recorded in which stones are thrown as if by invisible hands, heavy furniture is moved, and loud knockings are heard which frighten the life out of the unwitting victims of these curious 'ghosts'.

CHAPTER SIX

A South Seas Ghost

One Christmas Eve a man called Kimueli was murdered on the island of Rotumah in the Western Pacific. The murderer, an Australian, was caught and convicted. Before Kimueli died from his wounds he was seen by Mr H. H. Romilly, Deputy Commissioner of the Western Pacific area at the time. A piece of rough cloth was wrapped round Kimueli's injured head by way of a bandage, and the cloth was held in place by banana leaves.

A year later, Mr Romilly was again on the island, staying with a friend called Allardyce in a house quite near an influential islander named Alipati. Alipati – known as Albert to the Englishmen – was in the habit of visiting Romilly and Allardyce each evening to talk and drink with them. Just before Christmas, this routine was suddenly broken; Albert did not make his usual visits for two nights running. When his friends inquired about him, they learned that he was afraid to walk the two hundred yards that separated the houses because Kimueli's ghost had been seen walking there at night. 'Of course I laughed at him,' Mr Romilly wrote in his book, *True Stories of the Western Pacific*, and went on:

It was an everyday occurrence for natives who had been out late at night in the bush to come home saying they had seen ghosts. If I wished to send a message after sunset, it was always necessary to engage three or four men to take it. Nothing would have induced any man to go by himelf. The only man who was free from these fears was my interpreter, Friday. He was a native, but had lived all his life among white people. When Friday came down from his own village to my house that morning, he was evidently a good deal troubled in his mind. He said:

'You remember that man Kimueli, Sir, that was killed.'

I said, 'Yes, Albert says he is walking about.' I expected Friday to laugh, but he looked very serious and said:

'Every one in Motusa has seen him, Sir; the women are so frightened that they all sleep together in the big house.'

'What does he do?' said I. 'Where has he been to? What men have seen him?'

Friday mentioned a number of houses into which Kimueli had gone. It appeared that his head was tied up with banana leaves and his face covered with blood.

No one had heard him speak. This was unusual, as the ghosts I had heard the natives talk about on other occasions invariably made remarks on some commonplace subject. The village was very upset. For two nights this had happened, and several men and women had been terribly frightened. It was evident that all this was not imagination on the part of one man. I thought it possible that some madman was impersonating Kimueli, though it seemed almost impossible that anyone could do so without being found out. I announced my determination to sit outside Albert's house that night and watch for him. I also told Albert that I should bring a rifle and have a shot, if I saw the ghost. This I said for the benefit of anyone who might be playing the part.

Poor Albert had to undergo a good deal of chaff for being afraid to walk two hundred yards through the bush to my house. He only said:

'By and by you see him too, then me laugh at you.'

The rest of the day was spent in the usual manner. Allardyce and I were to have dinner in Albert's house; after that we were going to sit outside and watch for Kimueli. All the natives had come in very early that day from the bush. They were evidently unwilling to run the risk of being out after dark. Evening was now closing in, and they were all sitting in clusters outside their houses. It was, however, a bright moonlight night, and I could plainly recognize people at a considerable distance. Albert was getting very nervous, and only answered my questions in monosyllables.

For about two hours we sat there, and I was beginning to lose faith in Albert's ghost, when all of a sudden he clutched my elbow and pointed with his finger. I looked in the direction pointed out by him, and he whispered, 'Kimueli.'

I certainly saw about a hundred yards off what appeared to be the ordinary figure of a native advancing. He had something tied round his head, as yet I could not see what. He was advancing straight towards us. We sat still and waited. The natives sitting in front of their doors got closer together and pointed at the advancing figure. All this time I was watching it most intently. A recollection of having seen that figure was forcing itself upon my mind more strongly every moment, and suddenly the exact scene, when I had gone with Gordon to see the murdered man, came back to my mind with great vividness. There was the same man in front of me, his face covered with blood, and a dirty cloth over his head, kept in its place by banana leaves which were secured with fibre and cotton thread. There was the same man, and there was the bandage round his head, leaf for leaf, tie for tie, identical with the picture already present in my mind.

'By Jove, it *is* Kimueli,' I said to Allardyce in a whisper. By this time he had passed us, walking straight in

the direction of the clump of bush in which my house was situated. We jumped up and gave chase, but he got to the edge of the bush before we reached him. Though only a few yards ahead of us, and a bright moonlit night, we here lost all trace of him. He had disappeared ...

I had myself only seen Kimueli two or three times in my life, but still I remembered him perfectly, and the man or ghost, whichever it was who had just passed, exactly recalled his features. I had remembered, too, in a general way, how Kimueli's head had been bandaged with rag and banana leaves, but on the appearance of the figure it came back to me exactly, even to the position of the knots. I could not then, and do not now, believe it was in the power of any native to play the part so exactly ... the calm, quiet manner in which this figure had passed was, I believe, entirely impossible for a native playing such a part, and before such an audience, to assume. Moreover, Albert and everyone else scouted the idea. They all knew Kimueli intimately, had seen him every day and could not be mistaken. Allardyce had never seen him before, but can bear witness to what he saw that night.

I went back to my house and tried to dismiss the matter from my mind, but with indifferent success. I could not get over his appearance. We were so close behind him that if it had been a man forcing his way through the thick undergrowth we must have heard and seen him. There was no path where he had disappeared.

After that night, the figure was never seen again. But Mr Romilly, like so many people before and since who have witnessed such an event, could never forget the experience. It remained vividly in his memory for the rest of his life.

CHAPTER SEVEN

Some Australian Apparitions

Long before white men reached Australia the native inhabitants, the Aborigines, talked of the Bunyip. And when the white men came, the Aborigines warned them to beware of this old enemy of theirs. Mrs Campbell Praed, when writing about her experiences some years ago, called the Bunyip 'the one respectable flesh-curdling horror of which Australia can boast'. She meant that Australia is haunted by very few ghosts and ghouls compared with Britain and Europe; and she was right. Australia is an unspooky country, and most of the ghosts it lays claim to came, apparently, with the settlers, and with the Irish and Scottish colonizers especially. So the Bunyip is the oldest ghost inhabitant, and if it does exist, then Australians ought to be glad their country did not breed others as fearsome, as Mrs Praed's description makes clear:

The Bunyip is said to be an amphibious animal, and is variously described: sometimes as a gigantic snake; sometimes as a species of rhinoceros, with a smooth pulpy skin and a head like that of a calf; sometimes as a huge pig, its body yellow, crossed with black stripes. But it is also said to be something more than an animal, and among its supernatural attributes is the awesome, cold, uncanny feeling which creeps over a company at night when the Bunyip becomes the subject of conversation, especially if talk turns to the strange magnetic atmosphere supposed to envelop the creature. According to legend, it attracts its prey by means of this mysterious emanation, and when sufficiently near, will draw man or beast down to the water and suck the body under, and without sound or struggle the victim disappears, to be seen no more. It is silent and stealthy, and only rarely seen to rise partially from the black water which it loves, and utter a strange moaning cry like that of a child or a woman in pain. There is a theory that water is a powerful conductor for the kind of electricity it gives out, and that a pool with dry abrupt banks and no outlying morass is tolerably safe to drink from or to camp by; but a lagoon lying amid swamp has always an evil reputation, and in some districts it is very difficult to persuade a black fellow to venture into such a place.

One of the most famous haunts of the Bunyip, round which all sorts of stories gathered, though I could never really authenticate one of them, is a lagoon that we all knew well, and which used to furnish my brothers with many a brace of wild-fowl for our bush larder.

This lagoon is about four miles long, in some parts

very deep, in others nothing but marsh, with swamp-oaks and ti-trees and ghostly white-barked she-oaks growing thickly in the shallow water. The wild duck is so numerous in places that a gun fired makes the air black, and it is impossible to hear oneself speak, so deafening are the shrill cries of the birds which brood over the swamp.

We were none of us very much afraid of the Bunyip, though I confess to many an anxious shudder, and to having stopped and switched a stick behind me in order to make sure that all was right, when I found myself at dusk, walking by the banks of the lagoon. A curious fascination, which was assuredly not the magnetic attraction of the Bunyip, used to draw me there; the place was so wild and eerie and solitary, and appealed so strongly to my imagination. I liked nothing better than to go there with my brother on moonlit nights when he went down there with his gun over his shoulder to get a shot at wild duck; the creepy feeling which would come over us as we trod along by the black water with dark slimy logs slanting into it, and reeds and moist twigs and fat marsh plants giving way under our footsteps, was quite a luxurious terror. There were such strange noises, the faint shivering sound made by the spiky leaves of the swamp-oak, the flapping of the she-oaks' scaly bark, the queer gurgling 'grrur-urr-r' of an opossum up a gum tree, the swishing of the ducks' wings when they rose suddenly in the distance, the melancholy call of the curlews – all these, breaking the silence and loneliness of the night, were indescribably uncanny and fascinating; but I am bound to say that during these expeditions we never saw a sign of the Bunyip.

Mrs Praed's vivid description of that night-time scene not only brings to life the feeling of an Australian wilderness but shows just how many sights and sounds might easily have been mistaken for the dreaded Bunyip by anyone of a nervous temperament. Not that the Bunyip is entirely a far-fetched and fanciful invention. Around the world there are a number of aquatic and amphibious animals which, like the electric eel, kill by using electricity stored in their bodies. So maybe the Aborigine legend, like so many legends, is based on fact.

But the Bunyip is not Australia's only ghost. There are ones more like those that haunt other places around the globe. An old bullock driver told a story about a typical crisis-ghost, for instance. (A crisis-ghost is the apparition of someone who is in great personal trouble and it is usually witnessed by a relative or friend.)

There are ghosts, there's no denying; and I'll tell you of one that hundreds heard about, and many of you know the man who saw it, and you can ask *him* about it.

Many of you have been up the Murray [River] towards Albury, and have passed Brown's Station just above Quart-Quart. Well, when I was a government-man, I was doing my time near Camden, and in those days Brown had a farm at the Cow-pastures, close to where I was living. He had just settled down on the Murray with a few hundred head of cattle, and stopped there five or six months, so when he thought everything was going on well, he started for down-country, intending to bring up more stock in a short time.

He travelled on horseback, for there were no mail-coaches to the Murray then, and as he pushed on pretty sharp, he was very tired when he got to the Myrtle Creek. He told Thomson, the landlord, to call him early in the morning, took his supper, and two or three glasses of rum, and then went to bed.

Towards morning, something awoke him, and when he opened his eyes he saw his wife standing by the bed-side. Before he could speak to her, she told him to get up, and went out of the room at once.

Well, Brown was greatly surprised, of course, at seeing her at that place, but he thought that she had come to meet him, so he got up and dressed himself. When he went down, he looked in the parlours; but as he could not see her, he began to call out her name. At last, the noise he made roused the landlord, and he came and asked what the matter was.

'Why,' says Brown, 'I want my wife. She came and woke me, and now she's hidden herself.'

'You're dreaming, man,' cried the landlord. 'How can your wife be here? You know she's at the Cowpasture Farm.'

'What!' rejoined Brown. 'Do you mean to say that she did not come here after I went to bed?'

'Of course she didn't,' replied the landlord, 'for I locked the door when I went to bed, and the key is under my pillow.'

With that, Brown grew quite frightened. 'Saddle my horse at once,' said he, 'for so sure as I'm a living man, my wife came and spoke to me tonight, and I'm greatly afraid that something has happened to her at home.' With that, he mounted and galloped off.

He rode till he knocked up his horse, and then he borrowed a fresh one, and kept on as fast as he could ride, so that, before sunset, he came close to the Cowpasture Farm. As he galloped up, he could see there was something unusual going on, for several horses were fastened to the posts of the veranda, the working-men were standing in groups at the doors of their huts, and two or three troopers were lounging about near the stockyard. Brown jumped off his horse, and was going at once into the house, but one of his neighbours came out, and met him at the door. This gentleman led him away to a little distance, and told him gradually as he could what had taken place.

Now, Brown was a good master to his assigned servants, but his wife was a tyrant, and while he was at the Murray, she had been stopping the rations of the government-men, and sending them up to court. There was one man in particular she took a great dislike to; he could do nothing right, and almost every Monday morning he got his fifty lashes at the nearest court-house.

At last he got desperate. He was chopping some wood, when she came up to him, and after abusing him, said: 'I'll get you fifty more on Monday next.'

'I may get the fifty,' cried he, 'but you'll not live to know of it.' And with that he lifted the axe he had in his hand, and split her skull.

This happened at the Cow-pastures at the very hour when she was seen by Brown in the inn at Myrtle Creek; so you see, boys, there can be no doubt but ghosts do sometimes appear on earth.

Because the Australian Outback is such a vast and treacherous country, people have often lost their way in it and died from lack of food and water. Naturally, therefore, many of Australia's ghost stories are about such unfortunate folk. A man signing himself 'A Pioneer' told of such a victim:

One occasionally hears of some extraordinary phenomenon or apparition which at the time is not always to be accounted for, or, more generally, not believed, but that which I now narrate, though strange, I can vouch for.

It happened thus: At the end of a rather longer drought than usual, being called upon to attend a race-meeting to be held at Deniliquin, distant some thirty miles from my then residence, I started – taking with me a black boy, in order to ride a colt which I was breaking at the time, and myself riding its mother – when, crossing a plain about half-way distant from our destination, I noticed a peculiar clump of trees standing isolated in its centre; and seeing that the grass looked fresh I determined, on my return home, to send a flock of sheep out at once, to feed over this particular portion of the run. So, after participating in the events of the meeting, and being anxious to return home again, in order to carry out my resolve as to the moving of the flocks, I left the township about twelve o'clock at night, in company with my black boy.

There was a young moon, with a hazy and misty appearance, struggling through the clouds. We rode on, taking the shortest and most direct line for home, traversing the same country, mostly, that we had ridden over on the preceding morning; when, on reaching the plain with the circular stump of trees in its centre that I had previously noticed, I observed, at about a hundred yards distant, and near to the clump of trees,

the figure and form of a man, standing in an upright position, with his arms extended.

Though the moon at the time was partially obscured, and there was a dim and misty light, yet there stood out the distinct outline of the figure of a man; which I could not account for, knowing that there was no habitation or men residing anywhere within twenty miles of the spot.

On drawing my black boy's attention to it, asking him what he thought it was, his reply was, 'Baal, mine, know mine, think it devil devil, that fellow.'

His colt being the faster, and thinking it might be some unfortunate fellow who had wandered and lost his way, I told him to ride up and see; when, with a frightened accent, he cried out, 'Devil, devil, that fellow,' and, putting spurs to his colt, went off at full speed across the open plain, giving the clump of trees a wide berth; upon which, the mare, turning restive, started off after the colt.

The rest of our journey home I was puzzling and thinking over what I had so distinctly seen. However, the following day I made the necessary preparation for sending out the sheep, and, selecting an old and careful shepherd who knew the run, gave him particular instructions to feed this plain in the vicinity of the clump of trees.

Two days afterwards he made his appearance at the head station, having walked in, after yarding his sheep.

I thought something was wrong, or that he had come to report that his sheep had been lost or rushed by wild dogs; when he informed me that on feeding round the clump of trees as I had ordered him to, he had come upon the body of a dead man, lying on his back with his arms extended, and that from his appearance he must have been dead at least a month or six weeks. On his describing the spot where the body was, I at once recognized it as the same, and told him to return at once to his sheep, and that I would drive out in the morning and bring a spade and pick to bury the poor fellow.

On reaching the spot, there was the body of a young man, lying, as described, with his arms extended, and his head resting on a rolled-up blanket, who, from his appearance, must have been dead a month at least. Some cattle, seemingly, had been forming a camp round the body, pawing and scraping up the earth, as is usual with them on discovering any strange object. On his person there was a small pocket-book, containing a discharge from his late employment; and strange to say, his name was the same as my own.

CHAPTER EIGHT

An Indian Phantom

Of India's many ghosts those which most terrify their percipients are the agonized spectres of British men, women and children murdered during the Sepoy rebellion of 1857. Sepoys were Indian soldiers commanded by British officers and employed in a private army by the British East India Company to protect its trading interests. Discontent at the way they were treated was already unsettling these men when the rumour spread that the cartridges they had been issued with were greased with cow and hog fat. The Sepoys had to bite open the cartridges before use but the Hindus among them were not allowed by their religious laws to eat beef and the Moslems were not allowed to eat pork. So the order was the last straw. They rebelled, and for a year the slaughter on both sides was savage. Historians call the uprising the Indian Mutiny.

Typical of the ghosts seen since that time is one described by John Masters in his book *Bugles and a Tiger*, the story of his life in the Indian Army during the 1930s. Mr Masters had a friend, a cavalry officer, who lived in a bungalow which had been built before the Rebellion. One June night something woke this officer from a light sleep:

It was very hot, and the room was airless and oppressive, but he could hear no sound. An irregular flickering light played on the wall above his bed, as though a big fire was burning on the lawn. He got up and looked, but there was no fire outside. For ten minutes more the reflected flames crawled on his wall, and then they died. The next night the flames were stronger, and as he could not sleep he went out on the veranda for a smoke. He thought he saw two strangely dressed figures moving across the parched grass of the lawn. He thought both figures were armed, but when he went down to look there was nothing.

The flames did not come again, but he did find out that his big garden had once contained another bungalow besides his own. On a June night in 1857 two troopers of the Bengal Native Cavalry regiment then occupying the lines had crept across the lawn and murdered their adjutant there. It was the signal for the beginning of the Mutiny in that place, and an hour later the mutineers burned the bungalow to the ground as a funeral pyre for the bodies of the adjutant and his wife and two children.

Many of these pre-1857 houses had their ghost, says Mr

Masters, quite often the 'restless spirit of a woman murdered while flying from the scourge'.

Mrs Beresford was, however, the victim of a different kind of spectre: not a restless spirit re-enacting its sufferings of long ago, but an ogre intent upon an evil purpose among the living now. And it all but succeeded in its ugly mission. Was this malicious apparition raised by black magic performed by one of India's occult practitioners? Was it a demon of Mrs Beresford's disturbed imagination communicated telepathically to her daughter, who, as we shall see, also witnessed the ghost's final assault? Or was it a vengeful soul returned from the dead to take payment of Mrs Beresford for unknown injustices inflicted years before upon the soul's living body by some cruel white woman of the British Raj?

There are no certain answers to the puzzling questions raised by Mrs Beresford's story. All we surely know is that one day late in 1870 Mrs Beresford was riding in her carriage, driven by her husband, General Henry Beresford of the Indian Army, when she saw an Indian servant woman (an *ayah*) crossing back and forth in front of the horses. The *ayah* was old, dressed in dirty white clothes, and seemed determined upon being run over by the carriage.

'Stop, Henry, stop!' Mrs Beresford shouted, for her husband appeared to be quite unaware of the *ayah*

ahead of them. 'You'll run the foolish woman down.'

'What woman?' asked the General. 'There's no one in the way.'

'She's there, Henry, there . . .!' screamed Mrs Beresford. But too late. Horses and carriage drove over the *ayah* at that very instant.

The General had seen nothing, had felt nothing resembling an accident. But his wife was plainly upset so he reined the horses to a stop and climbed down to investigate. The road was clear, not a sign of anyone knocked down.

'You must be dreaming, my dear. There's nothing the matter.'

Mrs Beresford was incredulous. Had she not seen it all happen with her own eyes? The *ayah* walking dangerously across the horses' track, the horses catching up, knocking the foolish woman to the road and trampling over her fallen body. But here was her own husband telling her she had been dreaming!

More distraught than ever, the shaken Englishwoman climbed down from the carriage to see for herself. Sure enough, the roadway was clear; no trampled body lay bleeding under the carriage wheels.

'But I don't understand, Henry . . . I saw the *ayah*. I know I did.'

The General helped his puzzled wife back into the carriage and drove home, convinced the poor woman had suffered an hallucination caused by the effects of heat and tiredness. The couple had only just got back from a visit to England, and it always took a while to get used to the Indian climate again.

Hallucination or not, the *ayah* returned. Day after day for weeks on end Mrs Beresford was haunted by the tall, grubby figure of the old servant woman, seeing it now here, now there in the house. And as it slipped silently by, it grinned so evilly that she became convinced that the phantom meant to harm her. Unfortunately, the ghost usually appeared when Mrs Beresford was alone. She could appeal to no one to confirm what she saw. And slowly the ghost's constant appearances wore Mrs Beresford's nerves down till she was sick with fear and apprehension.

At last the General became alarmed at his wife's failing state of health and her daily claims that she had seen the *ayah*'s ghost again. A doctor friend was called in. He was no more inclined to believe Mrs Beresford's story than was her husband. What the poor woman needed, he advised, was a change. But they had just been away to England on furlough, the General complained; he could not possibly ask for more leave so soon. Then a nerve specialist would be needed, the doctor said; Mrs Beresford's condition was beyond an ordinary physician's ability to cure.

Mrs Beresford, however, would have nothing to do with nerve specialists. All she needed, she declared, was the company of her daughter, Barbara. She would lift her gloomy spirits and take her mind off the phantom. Accordingly, Barbara was sent for. Mrs Beresford threw herself into the distracting pleasures of preparing for the girl's arrival. The ghost kept putting in its appearances throughout the following days but so buoyed up was Mrs Beresford by the coming of her daughter that she managed to shake off the frightening effects of these spectral visits without too much trouble. When at last Barbara arrived, her mother was happier than she had been for weeks.

Mother and daughter spent their days together thereafter, and Mrs Beresford was pleased to discover that, though the *ayah* made itself visible as often as before, Barbara, like her father, could not see it and was therefore spared the horror of its ugly grin and the depressing gloom it left behind. Barbara was always aware of the ghost's presence, of course, because her mother would turn pale at those times and stare with glazed eyes into empty space. But the girl was sensible; she allowed the hallucination (as she too supposed it to be) to pass before continuing as though nothing unnatural had happened.

Then came a night when Mrs Beresford was woken from her sleep by the touch of bony fingers gripping her shoulder. The fingers were ice-cold and dug sharply into her flesh. She knew at once and with dread what awful hand held her in its grasp.

She opened her eyes, and sure enough the wickedly

grinning *ayah* was standing over her, the figure all the more eerie in the moon's dim light.

Mrs Beresford's hysterical scream woke the General. He sprang up in alarm, lit the lamp, and rushed to his wife's side.

But the phantom had vanished, leaving a shocked Mrs Beresford trembling in her bed. She tried vainly to explain what had happened: her husband would have none of it. Mrs Beresford had had a nightmare, he decided, nothing worse. All this *ayah* stuff was nonsense. She should compose herself and go back to sleep. True, there were red marks on her shoulder and they could have been made by the violent grip of a bony hand. But they might equally have been made by ruckles in the mattress . . . or any one of a number of perfectly ordinary things. What was more, the General warned, if Mrs Beresford went on waking him up unnecessarily he would sleep in another room so as not to be disturbed.

Night followed sleepless night. No matter how she tried, tossing and turning restlessly, Mrs Beresford's eyes stayed stubbornly open, keeping an unwilling watch for the *ayah*'s dreaded return. Finally, the General moved out of the room, his never very durable patience giving out as he had warned. In his place came Barbara, persuaded by desperate entreaties to keep her mother company by night as well as by day. She agreed to the request only on one condition, however. Her mother must see a local doctor, one who knew India from a lifetime spent living and practising there.

This new doctor's diagnosis was very different from the other's. Having heard Mrs Beresford's story from beginning to end, he did not dismiss the *ayah* as an hallucination or as a bad dream. There were Indian cults, he said, which used black magic. The *ayah* seemed to him like the kind of evil spirit raised by these magicians. Whatever it was, he believed Mrs Beresford would never be free of its attention until she challenged it.

'But what shall I do?' his patient asked, at a loss to know what the doctor meant.

'When it next appears to you, no matter how afraid you are, you must command it in the name of God to leave you. That is the only way I know that might exorcize such a ghost.'

If Mrs Beresford was cheered by the doctor's kindness – he had been the first man to take her story seriously – Barbara was more than a little disturbed. She had thought the doctor would simply dispel her mother's fears by diagnosing some quite ordinary tropical ailment. Now she found that, on the contrary, he had confirmed all her mother had said. She noticed, too, that when her father heard what the doctor had said he was quick to prevent any suggestion that he move back into his own bed where he would be ready to come to his wife's spiritual, if not physical, aid. Had

Barbara been a little more experienced in life she would have realized that it is always those who disclaim belief in the existence of ghosts who most fear them.

Luckily for Mrs Beresford, this 16-year-old schoolgirl was blessed with greater courage than her father. And for two nights all was well. Neither Barbara nor Mrs Beresford slept other than fitfully, despite the comforting glimmer of a night-light left burning on a table between their beds; but the *ayah* did not appear. By the third night Barbara was dog-tired and drifted into a deep sleep almost as soon as her head rested on the pillow.

In the middle of the night, the girl was woken by a strangled scream and the sound of a struggle coming from her mother's bed. She sat up and looked across the room.

For the first time someone else besides Mrs Beresford saw the ugly, grinning features of the ghostly *ayah*. The apparition was bending over Mrs Beresford's bed, holding the poor woman by the throat with its claw-like fingers. In vain Mrs Beresford was fighting against the phantom, trying with all the strength of desperation to tear the clutching hands from her neck. But the *ayah*, though it looked old and wizened, was astonishingly powerful.

Barbara was struck dumb for a fearful moment. Then she let out a terrified cry for help that pierced the night air and woke the household. At that, the *ayah* released its grip and turned to face Barbara. Never before in her short life had the girl felt such loathing as passed between herself and the ghost as they gazed upon each other at that moment. The *ayah*'s features were ghastly – hatred personified. Barbara tried to look away, tried to tumble out of bed and rush from the room. But she could not move a limb; she sat transfixed and helpless.

But the freedom Barbara's cry had won for Mrs Beresford allowed her to recover enough to summon the energy to speak.

'In God's name,' she groaned, 'be gone! Haunt me no more!'

For a second that seemed eternal there was a deathly stillness in the room. Then came a whirl of activity. The *ayah* sprang upon Mrs Beresford, lifted her from the bed high into the air with such ease that she might have been as light as featherdown, and flung her violently to the floor. At the same moment, the room door burst open, admitting the General and a crowd of servants. Before anyone could take in the scene, however, the *ayah* vanished from sight.

The malevolent ghost was never seen again. Mrs Beresford, bruised and shaken, was happily otherwise unharmed and revived quickly. The doctor called to examine her next day, and reassured the General, Barbara and, most importantly, the still shocked Mrs

Beresford, that all would now be well. Time proved him right.

Why the spectral *ayah* preyed upon such a harmless and gentle person as Mrs Beresford no one will ever know. But the Indian doctor's advice for getting rid of it seems to have worked. Usually, people who see ghosts are so taken aback that they lose their presence of mind. Whereas a few words spoken with determination and courage might well be all that's needed to free themselves from the apparition for ever.

CHAPTER NINE

Sea-Going Ghosts

A ghost to the rescue

One day, a sailing ship plying between Liverpool and New Brunswick, Canada, was off the coast of New-foundland when the first mate saw a strange man sitting in the captain's cabin and writing on a slate used for making rough notes in preparation for entering up the ship's log. The mate reported what he had seen to the captain, who would not at first believe him. How could a stranger be aboard? They had been at sea six weeks; even a well-concealed stowaway would have been discovered by now. Was the mate ill? Or drunk? Or had he been day-dreaming as he went about his routine duties? Scoff as much as he liked, the captain could not dissuade the mate. There had been a stranger in the captain's cabin, writing on the slate; the mate was convinced of it.

At last the captain agreed to go with the mate and investigate. The cabin, when they entered, was empty: no stranger, nothing disturbed or out of place, no sign at all that any unauthorized person had intruded.

Except for the slate. On it, four words were written in a hand neither the captain nor the mate recognized.

Steer to the north-west said the message.

Every man aboard was closely questioned; each was ordered to write the words, *Steer to the north-west*. But no one, from officers to cabin boy, could throw any light on the puzzling event, nor did anyone's handwriting even vaguely resemble the writing on the slate.

Completely baffled, and for no other reason than superstitious curiosity, which most seamen have in abundance, the captain ordered the helmsman to steer north-west. He had no idea as he did so what he expected to find, nor how long he would be prepared to maintain such a potentially dangerous course, for it led his ship directly towards hazardous ice-floes drifting down from the Arctic.

A sharp look-out was kept and a cautious press of sail rigged. And as it turned out, the captain had not long to sustain his patience. After an hour or so of plain sailing, an iceberg was sighted dead ahead, and alongside it, a battered and broken vessel bearing a starving crew and passengers.

A rescue operation was at once organized, the ship-wrecked survivors brought aboard, all of them exhausted from the effects of hunger and thirst and exposure to the elements. And it was while the first mate was helping a rescued man over the side to safety that he looked with amazement at the poor fellow's face. In every respect this was the stranger the mate had seen in the captain's cabin: no doubt about it – features, build, even dress, everything was the same as the mate vividly remembered.

At that moment the mate said nothing, but having settled the wretched man comfortably below decks and seen that their needs of hot food and drink, and fresh clothes were being supplied, he went at once to the captain to report his second extraordinary story of this extraordinary day. This time the captain was more willing to listen seriously to his first mate. Between them, they decided to call in the rescued captain and the stranger as soon as both men had recovered sufficiently to answer questions.

When the small party was eventually gathered later that day in the captain's cabin, the stranger – a passenger from the wrecked ship it turned out – was asked if he would be kind enough to write a few words at the captain's dictation. The reason would be made clear afterwards. The man agreed, and was asked to write, *Steer to the north-west*. This done, his handwriting was compared with that on the slate, which the captain had till then kept hidden from view.

The writing penned by the stranger and the writing on the slate were identical.

The surprised man found himself replying at once to a flurry of excited questions. His answers, added to by remarks from the rescued captain and completed by details recounted by his hosts, built into an incredible solution to the story of his and his exhausted companions' rescue.

It appears that after drifting for days in their wrecked boat, the unhappy survivors had all but given up hope of reaching safety. One man only remained certain that they would be found in time. During the morning of their rescue, this man had fallen asleep so deeply that the others feared he was slipping towards death, as others had before him. But after a time, he awoke and at once told the captain with entire confidence that help was on its way and would soon reach them. During his sleep, the man said, he had dreamed he was aboard a vessel that he was sure would come to find them. He even described the ship's appearance. That ship was the very one in which they now sat, and the man was the stranger the first mate had seen.

One curious detail remained to explain: the stranger remembered nothing about the slate. He had not, in his dream, sat at the captain's table writing a message. He had wandered about, looking here and there, and could describe what he had seen. But no amount of trying produced any memory at all of the slate and the call for help written on it.

What the mate saw, if we can believe this tale, was not the ghost of a dead man, but the ghost of a living man. And if that seems too much to swallow, consider this: in the annals of psychical research there are at least sixteen well recorded cases of men and women who deliberately set out to produce their own ghosts and succeeded. One of these is quoted in a fascinating book, *Apparitions* by G. N. M. Tyrrell (Gerald Duckworth). Those who doubt the possibility that a dying man's ghost can be seen and may even perhaps write a message on a slate, a message that leads to the man's rescue so that he does not die in the end, would do well to examine what Mr Tyrrell has to say.

The Flying Dutchman

Most famous of all sea-going ghosts is *The Flying Dutchman*, the phantom ship seen by countless sailors down the years, and the inspiration of legends, poems and music.

'Tis the phantom ship, that in darkness and wrath,
Ploughs evermore the waste ocean path,
And the heart of the mariner trembles in dread,
When it crosses his vision like the ghost of the dead.

So wrote the poet, Ayres. And indeed *The Flying Dutchman* is often taken as a sign of ill-omen.

There are several accounts telling how the story began. According to one Dutch legend, a certain captain had tried without success to round the notoriously dangerous Cape Horn against a head gale. But he would not give up and forced his crew to put on more and more sail, even though the gale was growing worse by the minute. All the while the reckless man drank and smoked and laughed with mad disregard for everyone's safety, including his own. Then came retribution. The Holy Ghost descended onto the vessel, no doubt with divine instructions to make the captain see sense. Instead, the crazed fellow fired off his pistol at the Third Person of the Holy Trinity, but managed only to wound his own hand, so drunken was his aim, paralysing his arm as a result.

This self-inflicted injury seems only to have added furious anger to drunken folly, for he cursed the Deity with unstinted curses and such vehemence that the Godly Apparition, its patience apparently exhausted by this crude master mariner, there and then condemned him and his luckless crew to sail *The Flying Dutchman* for ever without again putting into port and with nothing but hellish gall to drink and red-hot iron to eat and an eternal watch to keep. To this doomed captain was to be sent thereafter every worst sinner of the sea, every malicious mutineer, every coward, thief and ocean-going malcontent. Together these dregs of humanity would work an eternal passage.

Such was the evil entombed in that purgatorial boat that it spawned about it tempests, thick mists, and every kind of weather that seamen loathe. Thus it is that when you see the *Dutchman* scudding silent by, every sail billowed by a wind too great for a normal ship to raise a handkerchief against, you quake in your seaboots and wonder what dreadful fate awaits you over the next high wave.

In the lore of the sea, full of superstition and courage as it is, stories about phantom ships are legion. Of them the tale told by the second mate of the *Orkney Belle*, a large whaling steamer, is in many details typical.

One evening in the month of January, 1911, when we were about five miles from Reykjavik, Iceland, I was standing on the bridge with the captain, a thin mist swirling over everything.

Suddenly it thinned, leaving visibility easy, when to our surprise, a sailing vessel loomed practically head on.

The captain signalled dead slow and the carpenter bawled from the deck, 'The Flying Dutchman!'

The strange vessel slid slowly alongside, within a stone's throw, and we noticed her sails were billowing, yet there was no wind at all. She had a high poop and carved stern.

All our crew rushed to the side, but not a soul was to be seen on the strange vessel. Then three peals sounded as from a silver bell, when suddenly, this strange craft headed starboard and disappeared into the fog.

Maybe Boyles O'Reilly's poem *The Phantom Ship* passed through the second mate's head as he watched the ghostly ship, and especially this stanza:

> But heaven help the ship near which the demon
>   sailor steers!
> The doom of those is sealed, to whom the Phantom
>   Ship appears,
> They'll never reach their destin'd port, they'll see
>   their homes no more,
> They who see *The Flying Dutchman*, never, never
>   reach the shore.

The mate and crew of the *Orkney Belle*, however, somehow avoided such mysterious disaster and lived to tell their tale.

Whales with castles on their backs

One of the stories in *Further Stories from Lord Halifax's Ghost Book* tells of an old nurse who had a strange dream on two consecutive nights during the First World War. In her dream she saw what she afterwards described as 'whales with castles on their backs' circling round the third pillar of the Forth Bridge. The dream impressed the old woman so much that she wrote about it to her nephew who was at that time working on the bridge.

The letter was more important than the old nurse

could know. Her nephew was busy as one of a team of men fortifying the pillars of the bridge against damage by submarine attack. When he read his aunt's letter he felt sure the 'whales with castles on their backs' were nothing else but submarines described by someone who had never seen a submarine in her life. He showed the letter to the foreman, and he too agreed that it was very curious that such a dream should be reported to them just at that time. So the workmen were kept going day and night in order to finish protecting the pillars with concrete casings as soon as possible.

On the day after the work was completed two German submarines were spotted in the Firth of Forth, and did actually attack the bridge. Their torpedoes failed to cause any significant damage, and because the workmen had alerted the Royal Navy to the possibility of an attack, ships were standing by and one of the U-boats was captured.

Precognitive dreams – ghosts of sleep – are common. Many people experience them, and sometimes they can lead to such unusual action as this story describes. More usually, it is not till after the event dreamed about takes place in reality that the dreamer sees the importance of his night time drama.

Wilfred Owen's ghost

Wilfred Owen was one of England's finest poets; no one has better written about the horror of war than he. And it was a tragedy of war that killed him on 4 November 1918, only a few days before the First World War came to its end. By ironic mischance his family learned of his death on the very day of the Armistice, 11 November. His brother, Harold Owen, was at that time in the Royal Navy, a lieutenant serving in the light cruiser, HMS *Astraea* which was on station in tropical waters off Africa.

Lt Owen was very depressed, quite unable to enter into the happy mood felt by most people at the good news of the war's end. He thought he was suffering from the heat and the weakening effects of malaria. Nevertheless, he also felt something was wrong, something he could not quite identify. He was restless, uneasy, even thought of sending home a telegram asking whether his brothers Wilfred and Colin were well. But he decided against doing anything; the feeling was too vague.

It was in this 'mood' that Harold Owen saw his brother Wilfred's ghost some time *before* news of Wilfred's death reached him. The experience is described in the third volume, *War*, of Harold Owen's biography, *Journey from Obscurity*.

I had gone down to my cabin thinking to write some letters. I drew aside the door curtain and stepped inside and to my amazement I saw Wilfred sitting in my chair. I felt shock running through me with appalling force and with it I could feel the blood draining away from my face. I did not rush towards him but walked jerkily into the cabin – all my limbs stiff and slow to respond. I did not sit down but looking at him I spoke quietly: 'Wilfred, how did you get here?' He did not rise and I saw that he was involuntarily immobile, but his eyes which had never left mine were alive with the familiar look of trying to make me understand; when I spoke his whole face broke into his sweetest and most endearing dark smile. I felt no fear – I had not when I first drew my door curtain and saw him there; only exquisite mental pleasure at thus beholding him. All I was conscious of was a sensation of enormous shock and profound astonishment that he should be there in my cabin. I spoke again: 'Wilfred, dear, how can you be here, it's just not possible . . .' But still he did not speak but only smiled his most gentle smile. This not speaking did not now as it had done at first seem strange or even unnatural; it was not only in some inexplicable way perfectly natural but radiated a quality which made his presence with me undeniably right and in no way out of the ordinary. I loved having him there: I could not, and did not want to try to, understand how he had got there. I was content to accept him; that he was here with me was sufficient. I could not question anything, the meeting in itself was complete and strangely perfect. He was in uniform and I remember thinking how out of place the khaki looked amongst the cabin furnishings. With this thought I must have turned my eyes from him; when I looked back my cabin chair was empty . . .

I felt the blood run slowly back to my face and looseness into my limbs and with these an overpowering sense of emptiness and absolute loss . . . I wondered if I had been dreaming, but looking down I saw that I was still standing. Suddenly I felt terribly tired, and moving to my bunk I lay down; instantly I went into a deep oblivious sleep. When I woke up I knew with absolute certainty that Wilfred was dead.

Harold Owen's story is one among many of a similar kind recorded by hundreds of people over many years. Whether he actually saw the returned spirit of his brother or whether the apparition was some kind of telepathic communication from his distressed family, or indeed whether it was none of these but simply a vivid waking dream brought on by the tropical heat and Mr Owen's uneasy feelings and wonderings about his brothers, everyone must decide for themselves. There is no proving any of these possibilities. What we can be sure about is that though the legend of *The Flying Dutchman* might well be nothing more than a seaman's yarn, Harold Owen, the old nurse, and the first mate and crew of the *Orkney Belle* all experienced something no one dare dismiss. The difficult thing is to discover how to interpret what they experienced, to find out how those experiences happened and why, and what they mean. And that is the job of psychical researchers, not of story-tellers.

CHAPTER TEN

The Mystery Ghost of Amherst, Nova Scotia

When the trouble began, Amherst, now a county town, was no more than a large village, neat and trim and quiet. But in the summer of 1878 its rural peace was disturbed by a strange drama which, before it was played out over a year later, had become world famous. To this day the Amherst haunting remains Canada's most puzzling ghost story.

The time, then, is high summer, 1878; the place, a two-storeyed house on the corner of Princess Street and Church Street, a tidy building, painted yellow and with bright red geraniums blooming in the ground floor windows. Here lived a collection of people who, like actors in a play, each had their part in the real-life drama about to begin:

Daniel Teed, 35 years old, head of the house and foreman at the Amherst Shoe Factory – a respected, hard-working and well-liked citizen.

Olive, Daniel's wife, a sober, good-living woman.

Willie, aged 5, a strong, healthy lad with blue eyes and curly brown hair. His favourite pastime, it seems, was taunting the hens that pecked about at the back of the house.

George, seventeen months old, an intelligent baby and the village as well as the family favourite.

Two 'boarders': John Teed, Daniel's younger brother and a farm worker; and William Cox, Olive's brother and a shoemaker employed at Daniel's factory.

Under Daniel's care and protection lived two of his wife's sisters. They joined the household after the death of their mother and the remarriage of their father. They were Jennie (or Jane) Cox, aged 22, the village beauty and therefore much admired and courted by the local young men; and Esther Cox, aged 19, the central figure in the affair. Unlike her sister Jennie, Esther seems to have been very ordinary to look at: short in stature, plump, with a pale complexion and unremarkable features except for large blue-grey eyes that stared at you sometimes in an unsettling way. The village children liked her, and when she was in good spirits she could be kind and gentle. But when she was thwarted or out of sorts she sulked and was ill-tempered. Always she had a strong independent will and preferred having her own way.

A few days before the haunting began, Esther had had some unpleasant experiences. On 27 August, Daniel complained that for ten nights past his cow, which was kept behind the house, had been secretly milked, thus reducing the yield available for the family next day. Who could be the thief? Everyone knew that Esther loved milk and, naturally, suspicion fell on her. But there was no proof, so nothing was done.

That night, Esther had a vivid and terrifying dream, which she told Olive about next morning. In her dream she had been attacked by hundreds of huge black bulls with blood dripping from their mouths and feet made of fire. She was so distressed by the dream that she wanted Olive to go with her to a fortune-teller to ask what the dream meant. Olive, a good Methodist like all the family, would not hear of such a thing.

On the evening of 28 August the most distressing experience of all occurred. After supper, Esther's boy-friend Bob McNeal called and took her for a ride in a two-seated open buggy. It was a thundery night and rain soon began to fall. Well after dark, at about ten o'clock, Esther arrived home in a hysterical state, dishevelled and soaked to the skin. She would explain nothing of what had happened until a whole month later. She then claimed that Bob had taken her to a lonely spot and attacked her. She had been saved by the chance approach of another carriage, at the sound of which Bob drove off at a dangerous pace back to the village, where he dumped his girlfriend and dashed away, leaving the village there and then and never, as it turned out, returning afterwards.

Was Esther's story true? Did Bob leave Amherst out
of shame for his actions and fear of the consequences?
Or did something else happen about which Esther did
not want to talk? We do not know. What we do know
is that for days after the event she was speechless and
red-eyed from weeping.

Exactly a week after Bob's alleged attack, the haunting began. A foggy wet night sent everyone early to
bed. Jennie, who shared Esther's bed, was nearly asleep
when Esther asked if it was not the 4 September.
Jennie agreed that it was and told Esther to go to sleep.
From that moment the trouble started.

The only detailed record of the extraordinary story
was written by a Mr Walter Hubbell in a book called
The Haunted House first published in 1879. Hubbell
met all the family, even staying with them during the
last few months of the disturbances. Unfortunately, he
was not a very scientific investigator; in fact he was a
music-hall conjurer with an eye for a money-making
entertainment. His sensational book sold thousands of
copies and made him famous. We know, however, that
his account is carefully written so that the exciting
moments are made as dramatic as can be, and that some
of the things said by Esther and the others involved
sound 'stagey' and unreal – made-up in fact. Nevertheless, his record is fascinating; readers must simply
decide for themselves which parts are likely to be true
and which are not. This said, let Mr Hubbell continue

the story in his own fashion, joining him at the moment when Esther is lying in the dark, brooding on her misery.

The room in which the girls were in bed together was in the front of the house, in the second storey, at the head of the stairs, and next to the room occupied by Mr and Mrs Teed and their children, and had one window directly over the front door. They had lain perfectly quiet for about ten minutes, when Esther jumped out of bed with a scream, exclaiming that there was a mouse under the bedclothes. Her scream startled her sister, who was almost asleep, and she also got out of bed and at once lighted the lamp. They then both searched the bed, but could not find the mouse. Supposing it to be inside the mattress, Jennie remarked that they were both fools to be afraid of a little harmless mouse.

'For see,' said she, 'it is inside the mattress; look how the straw is being moved about by it. The mouse has gotten inside somehow and cannot get out because it is lost. Let us get back to bed, Esther; it cannot harm us now.'

So they put out the light and got into bed again. After listening for a few minutes without hearing the straw move in the mattress the girls fell asleep.

On the following night the girls heard something moving under their bed, and Esther exclaimed, 'There is that mouse again; let us get up and kill it. I am not going to be worried by a mouse every night.'

They arose, and one of them lighted the lamp. On hearing a rustling in a green pasteboard box filled with patchwork, which was under the bed, they placed the box in the middle of the room, and were amazed to see it spring up a foot into the air, and then fall to the floor and turn over on its side. The girls could not believe their own eyes, so Jennie again placed the box in the middle of the room and both watched it intently, when the same thing was repeated. Both Jennie and Esther were now thoroughly frightened, and screamed as loudly as they could for Daniel, who quickly put on some clothing and came into their room to ascertain what was the matter. They described what had occurred, but he only laughed, and after pushing the box under the bed, remarked that they must be crazy, or perhaps had been dreaming; and after grumbling because his rest had been disturbed, he went back to bed. The next morning the girls both declared that the box had really moved upward into the air, and had fallen to the floor, and rolled over on its side, where Daniel had found it on entering their room; but as no one believed them, they concluded it was no use to talk of the singular occurrence.

After breakfast, Jennie went to Mr Dunlop's to work (she was a tailoress), and the rest of the household set about their usual daily business, leaving Mrs Teed,

Esther and the boys alone in the house. After dinner, Mrs Teed sat in the parlour, sewing, while Esther went out for a walk. The afternoon was delightfully cool, a pleasant breeze blowing from the bay. Walking is very pleasant when there is no dust, but Amherst is such a dusty village, especially when the wind blows from the bay and so scatters the dust of the unpaved streets, that it is impossible to walk on any of them with comfort; and Esther, finding this to be the case, retraced her steps homeward, stopping at the post-office and at Bird's book store, where she bought a bottle of ink from Miss Blanche and then returned home. After supper, Esther took her accustomed seat on the doorstep, remaining there until the moon had risen. It was a beautiful moonlit night, almost as bright as day; and while seated there looking at the moon, she remarked to Jennie that she would surely have good luck during the month because she had seen the new moon over her shoulder.

At half-past eight o'clock in the evening, Esther complained of feeling feverish, and was advised by Mrs Teed and Jennie to go to bed, which she did. At about ten o'clock, Jennie also retired. After she had been in bed with Esther some fifteen minutes, the latter jumped with a sudden bound into the centre of the room, taking all the bedclothes with her, exclaiming:

'My God! What is the matter with me? I'm dying!'

Jennie at once got out of bed, thinking her sister had

an attack of nightmare; but, when she had lighted the lamp, was much alarmed at Esther's appearance as she stood in the centre of the room with her short hair almost standing on end, her face blood-red and her eyes looking as if they would start from their sockets, while her hands were grasping the back of a chair so tightly that her fingernails sank into the soft wood. And, truly, she was an object to be looked on with astonishment, as she stood there in her white night-gown, trembling with fear. Jennie called as loudly as she could for assistance; for she, too, was thoroughly frightened by this time, and did not know what to do. Mrs Teed was the first to enter the room, having first thrown a shawl round her shoulders, for it was a very chilly night; Danial dressed hurriedly, as did William Cox and John Teed, and the three men entered the room at almost the same instant.

'Why, what in thunder ails you, Esther?' asked Daniel, while William Cox and John Teed exclaimed in the same breath,

'She's mad!'

Mrs Teed was speechless with amazement; and they all stood looking at the girl, not knowing what to do to relieve her terrible agony. Suddenly, she became pale and seemed to be growing very weak, and in a short time became so weak that she had to be assisted to the bed. After sitting on the edge of the bed for a moment, and gazing about the room with a vacant stare, she started to her feet with a wild yell and said that she felt as if she was about to burst in pieces.

'Great Heavens!' exclaimed Mrs Teed. 'What shall we do with her? She's crazy!'

Jennie, who generally retained her presence of mind, said in a soothing tone, 'Come, Esther, get into bed again.'

As she could not do so without assistance, her sister helped her in, when she gasped in a choking voice, 'I am swelling up and shall certainly burst, I know I shall.'

Daniel looked at her, and remarked in a startled tone, 'Why, the girl is swelling! Olive, just look at her; even her hands are swollen. Lay your hand on her; she is as hot as fire.'

While the family stood looking at her and wondering what to do to relieve her, for her entire body had now swollen and she was screaming in pain and grinding her teeth as if in a fit, a loud report, like one peal of thunder without that terrible rumbling afterwards, was heard in the room. They all, except Esther, who was in bed, started instantly to their feet and stood motionless, literally paralysed with surprise.

Mrs Teed was the first to speak, exclaiming, 'My God! The house has been struck by a thunderbolt, and I know my boys have been killed!' She rushed from the room, followed by her husband, William Cox and John Teed; Jennie remained by Esther's bedside.

On finding the children both sleeping soundly they returned to the room and stood looking at Esther in silence, wondering what had produced the terrible sound. Going to the window, Mrs Teed raised the curtain and saw the stars shining brightly and all were then satisfied it had not been thunder they had heard. Just as she let the curtain down again, three terrific reports were heard in the room, apparently coming from under the bed on which Esther lay. These reports were so loud that the whole room shook, and Esther, who a moment before had been fearfully swollen, and in such great pain, immediately assumed her natural appearance and sank into a state of calm repose. As soon as they were sure that it was sleep, not death, that had taken possession of her, they all left the room, except Jennie, who went again to bed beside her sister, but could not sleep for the balance of the night, through nervous excitement.

The next day, Esther remained in bed until about nine o'clock, when she arose, apparently herself again, and got her own breakfast . . . At supper that evening the usual conversation occurred about the unearthly sounds, but as not one of them could offer explanation they concluded it was too deep a matter for them to talk about, and all agreed to keep it secret and not inform any of their friends or neighbours what had transpired. They knew that no one would believe that such strange, unknown sounds had been heard under the bed, nor that Esther had been so singularly affected from unknown causes. About four nights after the loud reports had been heard, Esther had a similar attack. It came on at ten o'clock at night, just as she was about to get into bed. This time, however, she managed to get into the bed before the attack had swelled her to any great extent.

Jennie Cox, who had already retired, advised her to remain perfectly quiet, consoling her with the hope that if she did so the attack would in all probability pass away, and she would then be able to go to sleep without further inconvenience. Esther remained perfectly motionless as advised, but had only been so for about five minutes when, to the consternation of both, all the bedclothes, except the bottom sheet on which they lay, flew off and settled down in a confused heap in a far corner of the room. They could see them passing through the air by the light of the kerosene lamp, which had been lit and was standing on the table; both screamed and then Jennie fainted. And was it not enough to have frightened any woman and made her faint?

On hearing the screams, the entire family rushed into the room; there lay all the bedclothes in the corner; Esther fearfully swollen, but entirely conscious, and Jennie lying as if she were dead. Indeed she looked like a corpse as the light of the lamp, which Daniel held in his hand, fell upon her pale face.

Mrs Teed was the first to recover her senses and, seeing that the forms of her two sisters were exposed, quickly took up the bedclothes and placed them on the girls again. She had no sooner done so than they instantly flew off to the same corner of the room, and the pillow, from under Esther's head, came flying through the air and struck John Teed in the face. This was too much for John's nerves, and he immediately left the room, after remarking that 'he had had enough of it', and could not be induced to return to sit on the edges of the bed with the others who, in that way, managed to keep the bedclothes in place over the girls. Jennie had by this time recovered from her fainting spell, and William Cox went down to the kitchen for a bucket of water to bathe Esther's head, which was aching, when, just as he got to the door of the room again with the bucket of water, a succession of reports was heard that seemed to come from the bed whence the two girls lay. These reports were so loud that the whole room trembled from their vibrations; and Esther, who a moment before had been swollen, assumed her natural appearance, and in a few minutes fell into an apparently healthful sleep. As all seemed right again the entire family retired, but could sleep no more that night.

The next morning Jennie and Esther were both very weak, particularly Esther. She arose, however, when her sister did and lay down on the sofa in the parlour. At breakfast the members of the family all agreed that a doctor had better be sent for, so in the afternoon Daniel left the factory early and went to see Dr Carritte, who laughed heartily when Daniel told him what had occurred, and said he would call in the evening, and remain until the following morning, if necessary; but did not hesitate to say that what Daniel told him was all nonsense, remarking that he knew no such tomfoolery would occur while he was in the house.

As the hands of the clock pointed to ten that evening, in walked the doctor. Wishing everybody a hearty good evening, he took a seat near Esther, who had been in bed since nine o'clock, but as yet had not been afflicted with one of her strange attacks of swelling, nor had any of the strange noises been heard. The doctor felt her pulse, looked at her tongue, and then told the family that she seemed to be suffering from nervous excitement, and had evidently received a tremendous shock of some kind. Just after he had given this opinion, and while he was still sitting by her side, the pillow on which her head was lying came out from under her head, with the exception of one corner, as if it was pulled by some invisible power, and straightening itself out, as if filled with air, remained so a moment, and then went back to its place again, under her head.

The doctor's large blue eyes opened to their utmost capacity as he asked in a low tone, 'Did you see that? It went back again.'

'So it did,' remarked John Teed, 'but if it moves

again, it will not go back, for I intend to hold on to it, even if it did bang me over the head last night.'

John had no sooner spoken these words than out came the pillow from under Esther's head as before. He waited until it had just started back again, then grasped it with both his hands and held it with all his strength, and he was, it must be remembered, a strong, healthy young farmer. However, all his efforts to hold it were unavailing, as it was pulled away from him by some invisible power stronger than himself, and again assumed its position under the young girl's head. Just imagine his astonishment! All the members of the family told me that they never saw any one so completely dumbfounded as John Teed was at that moment.

'How wonderful!' exclaimed Dr Carritte.

The doctor arose from his chair; and the loud reports commenced under the bed as on the previous nights. He looked beneath the bed but failed to ascertain what had caused the sounds. He walked to the door and the sounds followed him, being now produced on the floor of the room. In about a minute after this the bedclothes flew off again; and before they had been put back on the bed to cover Esther, the distinct sound as of some person writing on the wall with a metallic instrument was heard. All looked at the wall whence the sound of writing came, when, to their great astonishment, there could be plainly read these words:

Esther Cox, you are mine to kill

Every person in the room could see the writing plainly, and yet a moment before nothing was to be seen but the plain wall. I have seen this writing; it was deeply indented in the wall and looked to me as if it had been written with a dull instrument, probably a large iron spike. I say a dull instrument because the writing had a very uneven appearance, and the invisible power that wrote it was certainly neither an elegant nor an accomplished penman . . .

The reader can probably imagine their utter amazement at what had just taken place. There they stood around the bed of this suffering girl, each watching the other, to see that there could be no possible mistake about what they saw and heard. They all knew that marvellous things had taken place, for each had heard and seen them with his or her own eyes and ears. Still, they dare not trust their own senses; it was all so strange, so different from any previous experience they had ever had, or heard of others having had, that they were all, without a single exception, awed into fearful silence. The terrible words written on the wall – *Esther Cox, you are mine to kill*. What could their import be? Were they true? What had written them? All that was known was that they had heard the writing, and had seen the letters appear, one by one upon the wall, but there their knowledge stopped, and everything to their understanding was as blank as the wall had been before the invisible power, that threatened to commit murder, had exposed upon that smooth white surface the terrifying sentence in characters nearly a foot in height.

As Dr Carritte stood in the door wondering what it all meant, a large piece of plaster came flying from the wall of the room, turning a corner in its flight, and fell at his feet. The good doctor picked it up mechanically, and placed it on a chair; he was too astonished to speak. Just after he had placed the plaster on the chair, the fearfully loud pounding sounds commenced again with redoubled power, this time shaking the entire room and all it contained, including the doctor and other persons. All this time, Esther lay upon the bed almost frightened to death. After this state of things had continued for about two hours all became quiet, and Esther, poor girl, went to sleep. The doctor decided not to give her any medicine until the next morning, when he said he would call and give her something to quiet her nerves.

As to the sounds, and movements of the bedclothes and plaster and the mysterious writing, he could say nothing. He had heard and seen, and could not doubt his own senses; but had no theory to offer that would solve the unanswerable facts he had witnessed in the manifestations of some invisible power seeming to possess human intelligence of a very low and most demoniac type.

The next morning Dr Carritte called, as he had promised, and was greatly surprised to see Esther up and dressed, helping Mrs Teed to wash the breakfast dishes. She told him she felt all right again, except that she was so nervous that any sudden sound startled her and made her jump. Having occasion to go down into the cellar with a pan of milk, she came running up, out of breath, and stated there was someone in the cellar who had thrown a piece of plank at her. The doctor went down to see for himself, Esther remaining in the dining-room. The cellar stairs being directly under the stairway in the hall, the door to the cellar opened into the dining-room. In a moment he came up again, remarking that there was not any person down there to throw a piece of plank or anything else.

'Esther, come down with me,' said he.

They both went down; when to their great surprise, several potatoes came flying at their heads; and both ran up the cellar stairs. The doctor immediately left the house, and called again in the evening with several very powerful sedatives, morphia being one, which he administered to Esther at about ten o'clock, as she lay in bed. She still complained of her nervousness, and said she felt as though electricity was passing all through her body. He had given her the sedative medicine, and had just stated that she would have a good night's rest, when the sounds commenced, only they were very much louder and in more rapid succession than on the previous nights. Presently the sounds left the room and were heard distinctly on the roof of the house. The doctor instantly left the house and went into the street, where he heard the sounds in the open air.

On returning to the house he was more nonplussed than ever; and informed the family that when in the street it seemed as if some person was on the roof with a heavy sledgehammer, pounding away to try and break through the shingles. Being a moonlit night he could see distinctly that there was not any person upon the roof. He remained on this occasion until midnight, when all became quiet and he departed, promising to call the next day. When he had gotten as far as the front gate, the heavy poundings commenced again on the roof with great violence, and continued until he had gone about two hundred yards from the cottage, at which distance he could still hear them distinctly. Dr Carritte told me this himself. The next week it became known throughout Amherst that strange manifestations of an unknown power, that was invisible, were going on at Daniel Teed's cottage. The mysterious sounds had been heard by people in the street as they passed the house, and several accounts had been printed in the *Amherst Gazette* and copied in other papers. The pounding sounds now commenced in the morning and were to be heard all day. Poor Esther, whom the power had chosen as its victim to kill, always felt relieved when the sounds were produced.

About one month after the commencement of the wonders, the Reverend Dr Edwin Clay, the well-known Baptist clergyman, called at the house to see and hear the wonders of which he had read some accounts in the newspapers, but was desirous of seeing and hearing for himself; and he was fortunate enough to have his desire fully gratified by hearing the loudest kind of sounds, and seeing the writing on the wall. When he left the house he was fully satisfied that Esther did not in any way produce the sounds herself, and that the family had nothing whatever to do with them. He, however, agreed with Dr Carritte in his theory that her nerves had received a shock of some kind, making her, in some mysterious manner, an electric battery, his idea being that invisible flashes of lightning left her person and that the sounds, which every person could hear so distinctly, were simply minute peals of thunder. So convinced was he that he had ascertained the cause and that there was no deception in regard to the manifestations of the power, that he delivered lectures on the subject and drew large audiences. He always nobly defended Esther Cox and the family, when charged by unthinking people with fraud, and spoke of the affair often from the pulpit. The Reverend R. A. Temple, the well-known Wesleyan minister, pastor of the Wesleyan Church in Amherst, which the Teed family attended, also witnessed the manifestations. He saw, among other strange things, a bucket of cold water become agitated and, to all appearances, boil while standing on the kitchen table.

At this point in the haunting, Esther and her home became notorious. People flocked from everywhere to see for themselves the exhibition of ghostly activity. The police had to keep order, so big were the crowds day after day. Finally, such unaccustomed fame made Esther ill, and she was confined to bed for two weeks, during which time the disturbances ceased. She was then sent to a married sister at Sackville, New Brunswick, to recuperate for another two weeks, and again was unmolested.

So far there is little doubt that the haunting – clearly a poltergeist case – was genuine. But when Esther returned home, a fresh outbreak of activity produced some suspicious effects, and many experts believe that Esther herself was deliberately responsible for these frauds, probably in order to keep herself in the limelight. She was, after all, not very attractive and always overshadowed by her beautiful sister. She had undoubtedly received some kind of shock, as Dr Carritte realized, when out with Bob McNeal. So Esther was in low spirits and looking perhaps for attention and success. The haunting brought her both, and it was

quite natural, even if wrong, for her to try and keep
that attention and success for herself as long as possible.
Many other young people who have been the victims
of poltergeists have been tempted in the same way and
have ended up perpetrating ridiculous frauds on a
gullible public. Esther may even have been aided and
abetted by Mr Hubbell himself; he certainly put her
on public exhibition on one occasion and asked the
'audience' to pay money to see Esther produce her
ghostly effects!

Let's continue with Mr Hubbell's account from the
point where Esther returns from her sister's, and decide for ourselves whether the happenings after her
illness seem as genuine and believable as all that
happened before it.

On returning to Daniel's cottage, the most startling
and peculiar features of the power took place. One
night while in bed with her sister Jennie, in another
room, their room having been changed in the hope
that the power would not follow them, she told Jennie
that she could hear a voice informing her that the house
was to be set on fire that night by a ghost. The voice
stated it had once lived on the earth, but had been
dead for some years and was now only a ghost.

The members of the household were at once called
in and told what Esther had said. They all laughed
and informed the girls that no such thing as that could

possibly have been said, because there were no ghosts. The Reverend Dr Clay had stated that all the trouble had been caused by electricity.

'And,' said Daniel, 'electricity cannot set the house on fire, unless it comes from a cloud in the form of lightning.'

To the amazement and consternation of all present, while they were talking and laughing about the ridiculous statement the girls had made, as having come from the voice of a ghost to Esther, all saw a lighted match fall from the ceiling to the bed, having come out of the air, which would certainly have set the bedclothing on fire, had not Jennie put it out instantly. During the next ten minutes, eight or ten lighted matches fell on the bed and about the room, out of the air, but were all extinguished before anything could be set on fire by them. In the course of the night the loud sounds commenced again.

It seems that about three weeks after Dr Carritte's first visit to the cottage, Jennie stated that she believed that the power that made the sounds and lit the matches could hear and understand all that was said and perhaps could see them. The moment she had finished the sentence, three distinct reports were heard; and, on Daniel requesting Dr Carritte to ask the power if it could hear, three reports were heard, which shook the entire house. Dr Carritte remarked at the time that it was very singular. Daniel then asked if the power could tell how many persons were in the room, and not receiving a reply, repeated the question in this form, 'How many persons are in the room? Give a knock on the floor for each one.'

Six distinct knocks were instantly made by the power; and there were just six persons in the room at the time, they being Dr Carritte, Daniel Teed, his wife, Esther, Jennie, and William Cox; John Teed having left the room after poor Esther had buried her face in the pillow as she lay in bed, trembling with fright.

The family could now converse with the power in this way. It would knock once for a negative answer, and three times for an answer in the affirmative, giving only two knocks when in doubt about a reply.

This system of communication had been suggested by a visitor. And it was in this way that they carried on a conversation the night the matches fell upon the bed from the ceiling.

Daniel asked if the house would really be set on fire, and the reply was 'Yes'. And a fire was started in about five minutes in the following manner. The invisible ghost that had spoken to Esther took a dress belonging to her that was hanging on a nail in the wall near the door and, after rolling it up and placing it under the bed before their eyes, but so quickly that they could not prevent the action, set it on fire. Fortunately the dress was at once pulled from under the bed by Daniel, and the fire extinguished before any serious damage had been done to the material.

Daniel told me that when the dress was being rolled up and put under the bed, they could not see the ghost doing it. All was then quiet for the rest of the night; no one daring to go to bed, however, for fear another fire would be kindled.

The next morning all was consternation in the cottage. Daniel and his wife were afraid that the ghost would start a fire in some inaccessible place, where it could not be extinguished, in which case no one could save the cottage from burning to the ground.

All members of the family were now fully convinced that the mysterious power was really what it claimed to be, a ghost of some very evil man who had once lived upon the earth, and in some unknown manner managed to torture poor Esther, as only such a ghost would . . .

About three days after the ghost had tried to set the bed on fire by lighting it with the burning dress, Mrs Teed, while churning in the kitchen, noticed smoke issuing from the cellar door, which, as I have already explained, opened into the dining-room. Esther at the time was seated in the dining-room, and had been there an hour or more, previous to which she had been in the kitchen assisting her sister to wash the breakfast dishes. Mrs Teed was the first to recover from the shock, and seizing a bucket of drinking water, always kept standing on the kitchen table, she rushed down the cellar stairs, and in the far corner of the cellar saw a band of shavings blazing up almost to the joists of the main floor of the house. In the meantime, Esther had reached the cellar and stood as if petrified with astonishment. Mrs Teed poured what water the bucket contained (for in the excitement she had spilled more than half on her way down) into the burning shavings, and both she and Esther, being almost choked with smoke, ran up the cellar stairs, and out of the house into Princess Street, crying 'Fire! Fire!' as loudly as they could.

Their cries aroused the entire neighbourhood. Several men rushed in, and while some smothered the flames with rugs from the dining-room floor, others put them out entirely with water obtained from a large butt into which the rain water ran.

From this point on, the effects increased in number and oddity. Chairs and other furniture danced about the house, Esther was said to come downstairs 'seeming to fly', a curry comb followed her about, pulled along, some said, by a black string held by Esther! Of course, instances of trickery do not disprove all the phenomena and if only Esther Cox had been properly examined by qualified people and her affliction carefully recorded in a scientific manner we might today understand more about poltergeists than we do. Certainly, whatever silliness she resorted to towards the end of the affair, her story remains one of the most interesting and baffling of all such experiences.

Acknowledgements

The passage from *Journey from Obscurity: Wilfred Owen, 1893–1918* by Harold Owen is reprinted with the permission of the publisher, Oxford University Press; and the passage from *Bugles and a Tiger* by John Masters, with the permission of Michael Joseph Ltd.

If you have enjoyed this PICCOLO Book, you may like to choose your next book from the titles listed on the following pages.

Piccolo True Adventure

Other books by Aidan Chambers – thrilling and chilling!

HAUNTED HOUSES (illus)   20p

True ghost stories of some of Britain's most well-known houses and buildings. Spine-chilling and hair-raising, there are stories such as the ghostly drummer of Cortachy Castle which forewarns the family of a death among them, the spectral figures of the Garrick's Head, the grinning skulls of Calgraph Hall which always showed up when a party was on, and many other tales which will astound you and make you go UGH!

MORE HAUNTED HOUSES (illus)   25p

'. . . those eyes, along with the noiseless tread as the figure glided over the bare oak floor, gave me a sensation of such deep, deep fear as I shall never forget all my life . . .' Another excursion into the world of horror and dread with these true stories of hauntings, mysterious ghosts, unknown sounds and unexplained apparitions.

Some Ghostly Fiction

Geoffrey Palmer and Noel Lloyd
THE OBSTINATE GHOST
and Other Ghostly Tales (illus)   25p

Ghosts of all shapes and sizes flit through the
pages of this spine-chilling collection of spooky
tales. You'll meet a headless horseman, a pretty
Hallowe'en ghost and a ghost in a barrel —
not to mention the particularly *obstinate* ghost
that haunts poor old Cissie . . .

Alfred Hitchcock
HAUNTED HOUSEFUL   25p

Eight chilling stories by a master of the
macabre, whether it be in films, TV or the
printed word. 'First find a room where you can
be alone . . . turn the light down . . . (you don't
want to frighten the ghosts away do you?)
wait . . . a strange noise? . . . well, that's the
beginning and this is where I leave you . . .'
CAUTION: Not to be taken at bedtime.

More Piccolo Fiction

Penelope Lively
ASTERCOTE (illus)   25p

The Cotswold village of Astercote was wiped
out in the 14th century by the Black Death –
and its ruins now lie hidden in the murky
wood. But when Peter and Mair Jenkins discover it, and its secret 'Thing', they find themselves caught up in an atmosphere of medieval
superstition that becomes a frightening
reality . . .

THE WHISPERING KNIGHTS (illus) 25p

When Martha, William and Susie concoct a
magic brew, they unwittingly invoke the en-
mity of Morgan le Fay, the notorious enchant-
ress who is posing as the wife of a local tycoon.
She uses all her powers of evil against them,
and only the Whispering Knights and the
mysterious Miss Hepplewhite can save them
from a terrible fate . . .